SCIENCE, TECHNOLOGY, AND SOCIETY

NUCLEAR POWER AND ITS CRITICS

The Cayuga Lake Controversy

NUCLEAR POWER AND ITS CRITICS

The Cayuga Lake Controversy

DOROTHY NELKIN

Cornell University Press

ITHACA AND LONDON

First published 1971

International Standard Book Number 0-8014-0634-x
Library of Congress Catalog Card Number 70-147316

PRINTED IN THE UNITED STATES OF AMERICA
BY VAIL-BALLOU PRESS, INC.

Acknowledgments

This study of a controversy over a nuclear power plant proposed for Cayuga Lake benefited from the cooperation and assistance of many people. I am indebted to Richard A. Rettig, who guided the manuscript through several drafts and to Phillip Bereano, Harvey Brooks, K. Bingham Cady, Clarence Carlson, David D. Comey, Leonard Dworsky, Alfred Eipper, Charles D. Gates, James A. Krumhansl, Alonzo Lawrence, Simpson Linke, Franklin A. Long, Franklin K. Moore, Mark S. Nelkin, Ray T. Oglesby, Courtney Riordan, Jeff Romm, Carlos Stern, Peter Stern, and Thomas D. Wright. Several representatives of the New York State Electric and Gas Corporation cooperated in interviews and discusions and provided documentary material and extensive and detailed criticism of an earlier draft. Their help was invaluable in bringing perspective to the very broad technical and economic issues involved in the case. A Cayuga Lake Basin Planning Seminar organized by Leonard Dworsky provided useful background material. I also wish to thank Sidney Siskin for applying her considerable editorial skills to the preparation of the manuscript. I am indebted to the National Science Foundation and the Sloan Foundation for supporting the research and writing of this study.

DOROTHY NELKIN

Ithaca, New York
January 1971

Contents

Tables

Figures

Charts

NUCLEAR POWER AND ITS CRITICS

The Cayuga Lake Controversy

Introduction

In June 1967, the New York State Electric and Gas Corporation (NYSE&G) declared its intention to build a nuclear-fueled electric generating plant on the east shore of Cayuga Lake in the heart of New York State. A 725-acre lot adjacent to Milliken Station, the company's present installation on the lake, was purchased in early 1968 for $700,000. In February, the details of the projected Bell Power Station were described to the press. The 830-megawatt plant was scheduled for operation by mid-1973. The estimated cost was $135 million. Application for an AEC construction permit to build "Cayuga #1" was made in March 1968 and site clearance began in April.

One year later, activity on the application was postponed. What happened during this year is a story of controversy and opposition by scientists and citizens who perceived Bell Station, the first nuclear power station planned on a deep, stratified lake, as a threat to the primary water and recreational resource of the region.

The Cayuga Lake Bell Station controversy will be

developed here as a case study. Its context is one in which increasing need for electric power capacity conflicts with concern about the environmental effects of power generation. Many complex and widely relevant issues are embedded in the controversy. As new problems are posed by nuclear power and the increased size of generating units, the adequacy of the existing system of regulation is challenged. The case brings into focus relationships among scientists, public agencies, citizens' groups, and policy makers, and illustrates the problem of developing policy in the absence of appropriate standards and definitive scientific agreement on the character and dimensions of ecological damage. A major issue is the character of scientific evidence and its interpretation for policy purposes. What are the obligations of scientists with respect to interpretation of their data? How can inconclusive scientific data be used as criteria for policy decisions? How does the behavior of groups in opposition affect decisions concerning environmental issues? These are some of the questions raised where the siting of a nuclear power plant is under consideration.

The Cayuga Lake controversy is similar to many which are occurring throughout the nation as conservationists, citizens' groups, and public servants question the development and regulation of nuclear power. Indeed, public interest has reached the proportions of a social movement. An indication of this is the hundreds of anti-nuclear-power folk songs filed with the Library of Congress, one of which goes as follows:

On the mighty Mississippi, near Monticello, Minn.,
They're building a nuclear power plant and they're committing mortal sin,
They'll contaminate our river with radioactive waste,
With insidious poison that no one can see or smell or taste.

Monticello and Elk River may some day realize the fear,
That the radioactive fallout is getting in their beer,
Then the land of the sky blue waters will go down in history,
As the place where man perfected atomic dysent'ry.[1]

The Cayuga Lake case differs to some extent in economic and technological dimensions from other cases; but the basic issues, growing out of public demand for assessment of the broad-ranging effects of technological development, are ubiquitous.

[1] Mike Murphy's Hill-Dillies, *Atomic Power, Monticello Style.*

I / The Need for Power versus Environmental Concerns

Growth of the Power Industry

The plan for Bell Station was developed to meet the increasing demands for power in New York State, demands which reflected a national pattern of growth. In the United States, electric power loads have increased at an average annual rate of 7 per cent over the past thirty years, the consumption of power doubling each decade. In planning for expansion, the industry assumes that this pattern of growth will continue. Present capacity, located in about 3,000 separate plants, is about 300,000 megawatts. By 1990, according to one estimate, generating capacity will be about one million megawatts, and will require 492 new plant sites.[1] This estimate, assuming greatly increased size of individual power units, is based on technological developments in the power industry. In the 1950's, a 300-megawatt plant was considered maximum. The demonstration of the

[1] President's Office of Science and Technology, *Report on Considerations Affecting Steam Power Plant Site Selection*, December 1968, Chapter I.

technological feasibility of larger units rapidly led to a trend to larger size. For example, of the 3,000 existing power units, only 140 exceed 500 megawatts; but in 1967 the average size for new units contracted was 790 megawatts, and in 1968 this increased to 835 megawatts. Several 1,000-megawatt plants are now in operation or under construction.

The first nuclear power plant, at Shippingport, Pennsylvania, was developed jointly in 1957 by the AEC and the Duquesne Power and Light Company. With the

Table 1. AEC predictions of operating nuclear capacity by 1980 (MWe)

Year	Predicted capacity
1962	40,000
1966	80,000–110,000
1967	120,000–170,000
1968	130,000–170,000

success of this full-scale operation, AEC predictions of the growth of the nuclear power industry increased rapidly each year until 1967 (Table 1).[2] By September 1968, however, only fourteen plants, generating a total of 2,782 megawatts, were operable, and thirty-nine plants expected to generate 28,387 megawatts were under construction.

The disparity between AEC predictions and the ap-

[2] United States Atomic Energy Commission, *The Nuclear Industry* (Washington, D.C.: GPO, 1969), pp. 130–134.

parent pace of construction has complex origins. At first, nuclear power plants appeared to be more economical than fossil fuel plants in view of the trend to larger size units: of plants generating 800 megawatts or more, fourteen out of nineteen contracted in 1968 were nuclear fueled.[3] At the same time, they conserved disappearing fossil fuel resources. "Nuclear reactors now appear to be the cheapest of all sources of energy. . . . Nuclear energy will become cheap enough to influence drastically the many industrial processes that use energy."[4]

The nuclear power industry developed rapidly, and peak orders were contracted in 1967. In fact, contracts in this year alone were equivalent in megawatts to all prior years. During the peak in 1967, the AEC issued construction permits for twenty-three reactors and reviewed applications for twenty-nine.[5] The 1967 peak,

[3] President's Office of Science and Technology, *op. cit.*, Chapter I.

[4] Alvin M. Weinberg and Gale Young, "The Nuclear Energy Revolution, 1966," *Proceedings of the National Academy of Sciences*, 57, 1, January 1967, p. 1. Projections of the future use of energy and of the use of different fuels are provided in Pacific Northwest Laboratories of Battelle Memorial Institute, *A Review and Comparison of Selected United States Energy Forecasts*, December 1969. The *Review* differs from Weinberg's projection, in concluding that "the extent the nuclear energy will penetrate the electricity generation market is apparently very much in doubt."

[5] United States Atomic Energy Commission, *Annual Report to Congress for 1968* (Washington, D.C.: GPO, January 1969).

however, was followed by a marked decline in contracts, and in 1968 only ten utilities requested permits for thirteen reactors. (See Table 2.)

There were several reasons for this decline. Anticipated shortages in fossil fuel supplies did not materialize. More important in determining initial investment policy were general economic conditions—interest rates and the availability of money. Capital costs of nuclear power

Table 2. Central station nuclear power plants operable, under construction, or on order, 1953–1969

Date contract awarded	Number of units contracted	Size (MWe)	Estimated cost (millions)
1953–1965	23	8,580	$1,899
1966	20	16,044	2,411
1967	31	25,780	4,275
1968	17	15,642	2,978
1969	4	3,869	814

Source: United States Atomic Energy Commission, *The Nuclear Industry* (Washington, D.C.: GPO, 1969), pp. 131–132.

between 1965–1968 averaged $150/KWe, varying from $90 to $200/KWe, while fossil fuel plants, including smaller units, averaged $140/KWe. In the long run, capital costs are not the only determinant of whether a plant is economical. Utilities must weigh the higher capital costs of nuclear plants against the higher cost of fossil fuel. This is a complex calculation that must include interest rates and maintenance and operating costs; it is further complicated by the fact that coal prices may be adjusted artificially to create a competitive situation. NYSE&G management argued that, amortized over a thirty-five year period, nuclear plants are more economical than fossil fuel plants. With tight money, however, capital costs become an important factor. Capital costs of complex nuclear plant equipment are more susceptible to rising construction costs than those of conventional equipment. These costs were compounded as the large numbers of orders in 1966 and 1967 led to a delay in delivery time. In 1969, only two of the thirteen nuclear plants scheduled for commercial operation in that year were completed, bringing the total number of operating plants to fifteen.[6] The mean delivery time from contract to operation for the fourteen plants operating by 1968 was six years, ranging from four to ten years.

A new factor contributing to the decline in new orders, and a factor of increasing importance, is public concern with possible adverse effects of power plants. The credibility of both the AEC and the nuclear power industry in giving adequate attention to these adverse effects has been an issue in a growing number of controversies.

Siting Controversies

The planning and siting of new plants, originally considered largely in technical terms, has recently been complicated by a web of interrelated political, administrative, and social issues. A public which had once

[6] American Nuclear Society, *Nuclear News*, January 1970, p. 29.

viewed science as "some mysterious amalgam of philosopher stone, Holy Grail, and monkey gland,"[7] and technological development as unquestionable progress, has become highly sensitive to possible environmental damage caused by technology; and one focus of this sensitivity has been the nuclear power industry. Nuclear power, in particular, has generated controversy along with increased megawatts; and, as new power plants are planned and sited, local conservationists voice their apprehension. (See Table 3.)

Initially, objections to nuclear plants were based on the wartime connotations of nuclear energy and the danger of accidents.[8] Gradually, these objections have been compounded by more subtle concerns, based not so much on the possibility of accidents as on radionuclide discharge occurring during the course of normal day-to-day operation. Increasing opposition of writers, scientists, and political figures[9] has recently reached

[7] John Maddox, "Choice and the Scientific Community," in Edward Shils (ed.), *Criteria for Scientific Development: Public Policy and National Goals* (Cambridge: M.I.T. Press, 1968), p. 44.

[8] Public apprehension concerning the possibility of an atomic explosion is still strong. For example, the Columbia University Triga experimental reactor in New York City has never been permitted to operate, due to public concern (*New York Times*, March 2, 1970).

[9] See, for example, Sheldon Novick, *The Careless Atom* (Boston: Houghton-Mifflin, 1969). For a critique of the nuclear power industry see Dean E. Abrahamson and Richard E. Pogue, *Some Concerns about the Environmental Impact of a Growing Nuclear Power Industry*, Annual Meeting of the Minnesota Academy of Science, April 27, 1968.

Table 3. Siting controversies

Proposed plant	Size (MWe)	Dates		Primary issue of controversy	Current status
		Contract	Intended Completion		
Pacific Gas & Electric, Bodega Bay, California	313	1958	1964	Effect of proximity to San Andreas Fault	Canceled 1964
Vermont Yankee Northern Power Corp., Vernon, Vermont	514	1966	1971	Thermal and radiological pollution of Connecticut River	Will build closed circuit cooling system
Northern States Power Co., Monticello, Minnesota	545	1966	1970	Limits of radioactive release	State attempt to set standards more rigorous than AEC; suit in progress
United Illuminating Co., Westport, Conn.		Site purchased 1967; not contracted		Spoiling of recreational site	Site purchased by town for recreational area (canceled 1969)
Florida Power & Light, Turkey Point on Biscayne Bay, Fla.	652	1967	1972	Thermal pollution of bay and effect on fishing	Continuing controversy
Niagara Mohawk, Easton on Upper Hudson, New York	766	1963	1970	Effect on historical property, ecology of Hudson	Canceled 1968
NYSE&G Bell Station, Cayuga Lake, Lansing, New York	830	1967	1973	Thermal and radiological pollution of lake	Temporary moratorium in 1969
Portland Gas & Electric, Trojan Station, Portland, Oregon	1,118	1968	1974	Thermal pollution of Columbia River	Will build natural draft cooling towers

a point where the AEC is claiming that "growth in nuclear energy so urgently needed to meet the power requirements of the future [is] incongruously slowed down by public apprehension . . . despite the outstanding safety record of the nuclear power industry."[10]

Another source of controversy over the siting of nuclear power plants is the issue of thermal pollution. The dangers of thermal pollution are not, of course, unique to nuclear power. Nuclear plants, however, have been a focus of concern because of the growing size of generating units, and because they dissipate about 50–60 per cent more waste heat into the aquatic environment per unit of electrical output than fossil fuel plants.[11]

Conservationists see cause for immediate concern with the dissipation of waste heat into water. In 1968 the cooling water required for condensers in all generating plants accounted for three-fourths of the 60,000 billion gallons of water used in the United States for industrial cooling. Some projections suggest that, at the present rate of growth, in thirty years the electric power industry will have to dispose of about 20 million-billion BTU's of waste heat per day. This would require a flow of about a third of the average daily fresh-water runoff in the United States through power plant condensers.[12] The effects of waste heat on lakes and rivers—what is

[10] *New York Times,* January 31, 1970.

[11] For an explanation of this difference, see p. 25.

[12] John R. Clark, "Thermal Pollution and Aquatic Life," *Scientific American,* 200, 3, March 1969, pp. 119–127.

commonly called "thermal pollution"—is a controversial subject to be discussed in detail in later sections.

Utility spokesmen claim that conservationist opposition is a major factor in electric power shortage.[13] It is premature to estimate how much delay is, in fact, caused by public controversy. A survey was made by John F. Hogerton of S. M. Stoller Corporation of the delays experienced by seventy nuclear plants for which construction permit applications had been submitted.[14] Average slippage in the expected schedule was 4.5 months, ranging from one to thirteen months. Causes of delay in order of importance were: labor, licensing, delivery, public opposition, construction problems, scheduling factors, and other factors. Hogerton claims that public opposition is not a major source of delay at present, but threatens to become one in the future. He also pointed to indirect effects of public opposition. Although only sixteen utilities claimed public opposition to be a major factor in delay, public pressure was seen by Hogerton as affecting the cost of nuclear power by involving the utilities in increased ecological research and planning for aesthetic considerations. Moreover, public opposition has created a climate "conducive to ultra conservatism in the setting of licensing requirements." The extent to which these requirements have tightened is still not clear, but it is evident that controversy has immensely complicated the task of permit-issuing agencies.

[13] *New York Times*, February 3, 1970, and *Electric Utility Industry and Environment* (Albany, 1968).

[14] *Nuclear Industry*, February 1970, pp. 20–22.

This is apparent in the Cayuga Lake case. Before examining the details, let us look at one further aspect of the context in which the case developed, namely the administrative network which regulates and controls construction of nuclear-fueled power stations.

Regulated Electric Power

The electric power industry is composed of regulated monopolies. In New York State, they are controlled primarily through the Public Service Commission (PSC), an agency which regulates the rates utilities may charge consumers and assures the adequacy of service. Though not directly involved in issuing permits, the PSC is concerned that utilities expand in order to provide adequate service at minimum cost.[15] Thus it regularly assesses utility planning and expenditure.

Fossil fuel plants require one major permit—a discharge permit—which is obtained from the New York State Department of Health. Three major permits, by comparison, are required for the construction and operation of a nuclear power plant: a construction permit and an operating license from the AEC, and a discharge permit from the State Department of Health (see Table 4).

Nuclear power plants are presently licensed under the 1954 Atomic Energy Act, Section 104B—that is, as development rather than as commercial reactors. This is an interesting legal point. The statute provides for the

[15] Public Service Commission, *Annual Report*, 1967, p. 31.

existence of a commercial reactor program. Though reactors are developed to the stage that they are sold as commercial equipment, no reactor to date has been regarded by the AEC as being in a commercial category for purposes of licensing. This has antitrust implications

Table 4. Major required permits for a nuclear power plant in New York State

Permit	Granting agency	Sphere of authority	Avenues for public participation
Construction permit *	AEC	Radiological safety	Mandatory hearings
Discharge permit	New York State Department of Health †	Thermal pollution	Hearings (not mandatory)
Operating license	AEC	Radiological safety	Hearings (not mandatory)
To charge consumer	Public Service Commission	Consumer rates	Hearings (not mandatory)

* As a development (i.e., noncommercial) reactor.
† Guided by standards established by the State Water Resources Commission and approved by the Federal Water Pollution Control Administration.

which have become a political issue (see pp. 110–116).

The licensing procedure begins with an application for a construction permit to the Division of Reactor Licensing of the AEC. A preliminary safety analysis report is submitted to the division, which reviews the application and specifications, explores questionable areas, and requests the Advisory Committee on Reactor Safeguards [16] to review the safety analysis. A hearing is conducted by the Atomic Safety and Licensing Board at the proposed site, and if the plant design meets existing radiological safety standards as established by the AEC rules and regulations, the permit is provided. This phase of the licensing procedure often takes more than a year.

The AEC also must grant an operating license when the facility is completed, but a hearing at this time is not mandatory. Other federal agencies, such as the Fish and Wildlife Service of the Department of the Interior, may advise the AEC on specific issues; however, they cannot formally influence the licensing decision. For example, on October 11, 1968, a commissioner of the Fish and Wildlife Service wrote a letter to the Director of Regulations of the AEC, providing information about risks to aquatic life and urging their consideration: "We understand the regulatory authority of the Atomic Energy Commission is confined to consideration of . . . radiological health and safety. However, we recommend and urge that, before a permit is issued, the effects of thermal discharge . . . be called to the attention of the applicant." [17]

The AEC has regarded its mandate as limited to ra-

[16] A statutory committee established by Congress in 1957 by an amendment to the Atomic Energy Act of 1954.

[17] Relationships between the AEC and the Department of Interior on these issues were clarified in a "memorandum of understanding" signed by both Stewart Udall and Glenn Seaborg in March 1964. This appears in U.S. Senate, Committee on

diological health and safety. Although often urged to consider thermal effects of power plant discharge, the AEC position, consistent with its original goals, and supported by the Department of Justice, is that they have no jurisdiction in this area.[18]

In the State of New York, thermal standards are controlled by the New York State Department of Health through its authority to issue discharge permits. The task of the health department has been immensely complicated by the increasing size of power plants; and the new dimensions of the thermal pollution problem require a more sophisticated technical expertise. The health department operates in accordance with criteria set by the State Water Resources Commission, established by the governor in 1965 to coordinate water research planning and to assign water quality standards. Other state agencies, such as the Department of Conservation, may advise on problems relating to the effect

Public Works, *Thermal Pollution, Hearings*, 90th Congress, 2nd Session, 1968, pp. 999–1000.

[18] The limits of the AEC authority were confirmed by Circuit Judge Coffin in September 1969, *State of New Hampshire* v. *Atomic Energy Commission* 406 F. 2d 170 (1969). The situation changed in March 1970. To comply with the Environmental Policy Act (Jackson Act) requiring federal agencies to take environmental factors into account, the AEC announced that it would require applicants to show clearance from appropriate authorities on nonradiation environmental matters. Pending is a bill proposed by Senator Edmund Muskie (Democrat of Maine) to give the AEC broad jurisdiction over thermal discharge (*Nucleonics Week*, March 12 and March 19, 1970). See also United States Atomic Energy Commission, *Annual Report*, p. 120.

of water quality on fish, animal and plant resources, but they have no permit-issuing power.[19]

The health department must, however, review its policies with the Federal Water Pollution Control Administration (FWPCA). Federal guidelines for thermal effects on lakes recommend a maximum of 5° F. effect beyond a permitted mixing zone, the size of which has been left ambiguous. Arguments as to the size of this zone have ranged from several hundred feet to ten miles,[20] and there is considerable variation from state to state. Nevertheless, the FWPCA has implicit power which may be exercised in the Cayuga Lake case with respect to the 1969 recommendations of the Water Resources Commission in New York State. These allow increases in the surface temperature of waters of no more than 3° F. beyond a radius of 300 feet from a discharge point. Conservationists are hoping that, despite the ambiguity of its guidelines, the FWPCA will insist on more rigorous standards for lakes when it reviews the commission's recommendations.[21]

[19] Governor Rockefeller proposed changes in the state organization in March 1970 which would establish a central agency, the Department of Environmental Conservation, to coordinate the administration of environmental and resource programs. However, the new department is not organized to cope with the inadequacies of the present system, since enforcement procedures would not be altered.

[20] Clark, *op. cit.*, p. 26.

[21] The recent FWPCA hearings and litigation in Florida concerning the prospective damage to Biscayne Bay due to thermal pollution by the Florida Power and Light Turkey Bay power plant set an interesting precedent. The FWPCA entered this

This is the broad context in which the Cayuga Lake case developed. Its unfolding reveals the scientific, economic and political issues intrinsic in a conflict between growing power needs and environmental concerns.

case at the request of Governor Kirk (*New York Times*, February 25, 1970).

II / *The Local Context*

The Lake

Cayuga Lake is the second largest of Central New York State's Finger Lakes and the second deepest lake, excluding the Great Lakes, east of the Rocky Mountains. Formed during the Pleistocene glacial advances, the lake has the following physical features:

Elevation	382 feet
Area	66 square miles
Length	38 miles
Mean width	1.8 miles
Maximum depth	435 feet
Mean depth	179 feet
Volume	331 billion cubic feet
Average through flow	1000 cubic feet per second
Flushing time	About 9–12 years

The extent of concern with the effects of the power station rests on the limited past experience with the particular technical problems involved in placing a reactor on a slow flushing inland lake. The potential problem has to do with the thermal stratification pattern of deep lakes.[1] Cayuga Lake has an annual thermal cycle consisting essentially of two stratification periods. From about the first week in May to the first week in December (about two hundred days, with a normal annual variation of up to fifteen days) the lake is stratified into three areas: the epilimnion or surface layer, the hypolimnion or deepest and coldest layer, and the metalimnion or intermediate layer (see Figure 1). During the

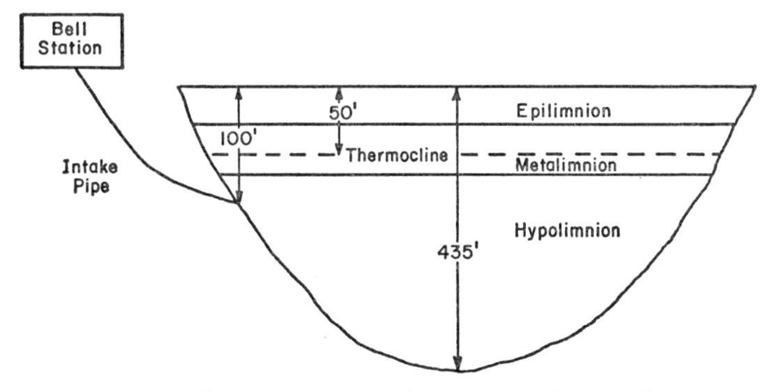

Figure 1. Stratification pattern of Cayuga Lake at midsummer

second period, from December to May, the lake is isothermal.[2] As the lake loses heat in the winter and temperature differences between the levels decrease, mixing occurs and the lake reaches a uniform temperature of about 35°–40° F. Again, in the spring, as heat is gained at the surface, it is vertically diffused; but temperature

[1] For technical information concerning the lake, see E. B. Henson *et al.*, *The Physical Limnology of Cayuga Lake*, Cornell University Agricultural Experiment Station, Memoir 378 (August 1961).

[2] Some limnologists use the term "homothermous."

changes decrease with the depth of the water. The hypolimnion is never warmed above about 45° F. The maximum rate of change occurs at a level called the thermocline, a mixing barrier which varies in depth seasonally and beyond which thermal mixing essentially ceases. Since the colder water in the hypolimnion has a greater density than the warmer water of the upper layers, thermal stratification tends to be maintained until temperature differences between levels decrease again with the cold winter months.

The behavior of the lake affects the distribution of oxygen and nutrients. During the stratification period, the oxygen content of the hypolimnion decreases. The thermocline shields the transfer of oxygen from the epilimnion. Since there are no mechanisms other than molecular diffusion to provide transfer, the normal respiration of crustacea and other organisms, as well as aerobic bacterial rotting, reduce the existing supply of oxygen in this lower layer. Oxygen is annually replenished during the winter mixing period.

The hypolimnion also stores concentrations of excess phosphorous and other nutrients fed to the lake by runoff from the drainage area. Algae in the upper layers of the lake feed on phosphorous, and when the algae die and settle, they carry nutrients with them. The algae decay and phosphorous is released, concentrating in the hypolimnion and the bottom sediments, where it does not contribute to plant growth. In this way, some nutrients are removed from the epilimnion, helping to reduce plant activity during the summer.

The Reactor

The NYSE&G ordered a General Electric boiling water reactor. This generates electrical energy through the following process. Water is pumped into a reactor vessel where there are fuel rods containing slightly enriched uranium. A neutron chain-reaction occurring in

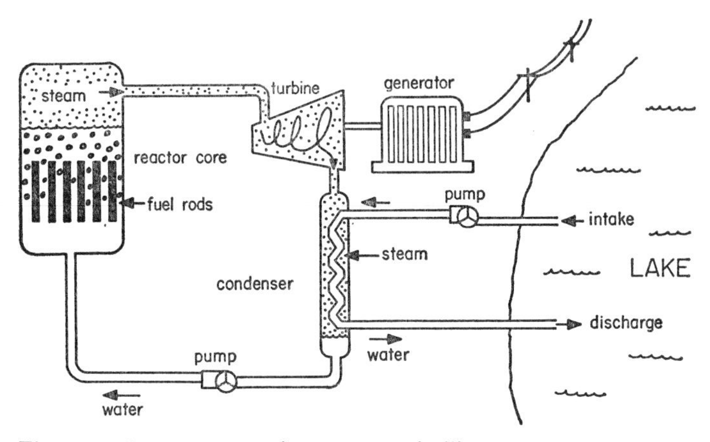

Figure 2. Power generating system—boiling water reactor
Adapted from Ray L. Lyerly and Walter Mitchell, *Nuclear Power Plants* (USAEC, 1967), pp. 6, 7, 16.

the fuel element produces the heat. The heat boils water flowing through the reactor, and the resultant steam drives a turbine generator (see Figure 2). Spent steam is converted back to water by condensers.

The condensers of Bell Station were designed for about a 20° F. rise in cooling water,[3] so that the water

[3] The NYSE&G indicated that this decision was tentative, and was later to claim that critics were premature in taking issue with tentative plans.

pumped in from the hypolimnion, a hundred feet below the surface at a temperature of about 45° F., would be discharged on the surface at about 65° F. The reactor, generating 830 megawatts, would circulate about 1,225 cubic feet of cooling water per second, and the maximum rate of heat discharged would be 5.55 billion BTU's per hour. This is about 50–60 per cent more waste heat per electrical kilowatt dissipated into cooling water than would be released by a typical fossil fuel plant of equivalent size.[4]

There are several reasons for this difference. Nuclear plants operate at about 7 per cent lower thermal efficiency than modern fossil fuel plants because they cannot run at as high a temperature. Furthermore, all the waste heat in nuclear units is dissipated through the condenser cooling water, while fossil fuel plants release about 15 per cent of their waste heat up a stack.[5]

The availability of year-round cold water from the hypolimnion is a considerable advantage to the utility. Condensers are a significant expense, and their size is a

[4] Milliken Station has two fossil fuel units generating 300 megawatts and circulating 376 cubic feet per second of cooling water. The water is discharged at 15° F. increase in temperature, and the rate of heat discharged is 1.3 billion BTU's per hour.

[5] A typical modern fossil fuel plant approaches an efficiency of 40 per cent, that is, for every forty units of electric energy there are sixty units of waste heat. Ten of these are dissipated through a boiler stack as heated gases, and fifty are discharged into the condenser cooling water. The expected efficiency of Bell Station was, at most, 33 per cent. More typically, the efficiency of water-moderated nuclear plants is 25–30 per cent,

function of the temperature of the available cooling water. The particular configuration of Cayuga Lake, with cold water available year round, would permit the use of a relatively small and inexpensive condenser.

The New York State Electric and Gas Corporation[6]

Incorporated as the Ithaca Gas Company in 1852, the New York State Electric and Gas Corporation (NYSE&G) was organized along its present lines during the period of utility amalgamations in the 1920's and 1930's. Two hundred and forty local companies were consolidated, and by 1937 the company's service extended to its present territory of 17,000 square miles, or 35 per cent of New York State's land area (see Figure 3). Today the company is governed by a board of directors and owned by 18,200 stockholders. It employs 3,636 people, 550 of whom work in Tompkins County.

and all the waste heat is discharged into the cooling water. Using the conservative estimate of 33 per cent, the ratio of "thermal pollution" to electric energy in each case can be calculated as follows:

Bell Station $$\frac{\text{Thermal pollution}}{\text{Electric energy}} = \frac{67}{33} = 2$$

Fossil fuel plants $$\frac{\text{Thermal pollution}}{\text{Electric energy}} = \frac{50}{40} = 1.25$$

These numbers indicate that while a nuclear plant is only about 7 per cent (40–33 per cent) less efficient than a fossil fuel plant, it causes 60 per cent more thermal pollution.

[6] New York State Electric and Gas Corporation, *Annual Reports*, and *Electrical World: Directory of Utilities* (New York: McGraw-Hill, 1968).

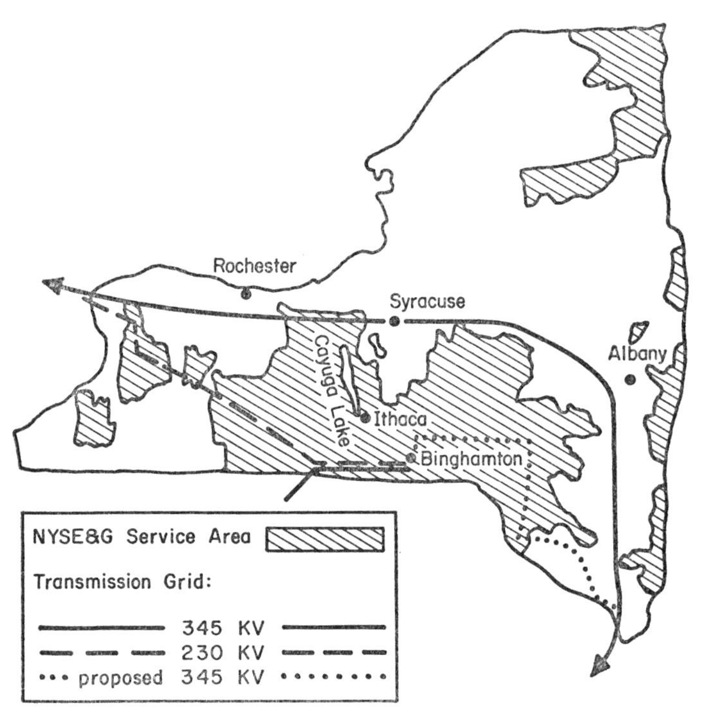

Figure 3. New York State EHV transmission grid and service area of the New York State Electric and Gas Corporation

Adapted from *Report of the Public Service Commission,* 1967, p. 32; 1968, p. 33.

The NYSE&G provides primarily rural residential service to about 10 percent of the state's population—537,875 consumer units in 1968. In contrast to other utilities in the state which service a large number of industrial customers, only about 19 per cent of NYSE&G power is sold for industrial purposes, one of its largest customers being Cornell University.

The utility's operation and maintenance expenses, excluding capital costs, totaled 54,163,000 in 1968. Production costs, including the price of coal, made up 54 per cent of this amount; operating costs (transmission, distribution, customer accounting, sales promotion, and administration) 46 per cent.

The distribution of residential, commercial, and industrial customers, and data on electric sales in 1968, are shown in Table 5.

Table 5. NYSE&G electric sales, 1968*

Customer	Number of customers (average for year)	Average use (KW-hr.)	Sales revenues † per KW-hr. (cents)	Annual average bill (dollars)
Residential	480,197	5,111	2.55	130
Commercial	49,405	27,336	1.99	543
Industrial	1,238	1,507,999	1.09	16,435
Other	7,035			

* NYSE&G *Annual Report*, 1968.

† In addition, there is revenue from street lighting at 4.3¢ per KW-hr., 1.30¢ per KW-hr. from other electric utilities, and 1.48¢ per KW-hr. from public authorities.

In 1968, the peak load was 1,308 megawatts. Total system capability was 1,399 megawatts, of which 854 megawatts were from company-owned facilities and 545 megawatts were purchased from the New York State Power Authority. This power is purchased under long-term contracts expiring in 1985 and 1990. Cost of the electricity is determined by a formula which provides for the utility to pay the Power Authority specified amounts for energy and capacity and which also requires NYSE&G to pass on to its customers any savings resulting from the purchase of this electricity. In 1968, NYSE&G paid 4.82 mills per kw-hr. for the total amount purchased, and it returned to its customers $780,000 as "savings," making the actual cost of power 5.05 mills per kw-hr for that year.[7]

In 1969 a 1,280-megawatt station at Homer City, Pennsylvania, was completed. Owned jointly by the NYSE&G and the Pennsylvania Electric Company, this added 640 megawatts to the company's generating capacity. The Bell Station addition of 830 megawatts would represent a 55 per cent increase in the NYSE&G net generating capability including the Homer City plant output. It is thus of considerable importance in the company's planning.

The utility operates as a part of the New York State Power Pool, and its lines tie into the Northeast Pool and the Pennsylvania, New Jersey, and Maryland Pool. Within the New York State Power Pool, there is a continuing exchange of power; companies with a surplus will provide kilowatts to areas outside their territory, balancing through exchange or reimbursement.

Expansion of facilities is felt to be necessary and desirable to the NYSE&G for several reasons. First, it

[7] 4.82 mills per KW-hr. is a very advantageous rate. When capital costs are included in the estimates of power production, nuclear power generation is usually estimated to cost about 8 mills per KW-hr.

allows the company to maintain its share of the state's system of distribution. Second, it enables the company to provide service as required by law to new units within its territory. Utilities are obliged to extend their distribution lines up to 1,500 feet from the end of an existing line for new customers. Third, although the NYSE&G is not as sensitive to economic fluctuation as other utilities (such as Niagara Mohawk, which distributes 51 per cent of its power to industry), it anticipates, on the basis of its own history, a 6–7 per cent annual increase in electricity demand.[8] This prediction is buttressed by data from the New York State Office of Planning Coordination on population growth, increase in the number of households and businesses, and technological development. On the basis of these data, the major utilities and the Power Authority in New York State planned to add 10,000 megawatts of generating capacity between 1968 and 1973.[9]

A further source of pressure to expand is the existence of the New York State Power Authority, a state-owned utility which may generate power and sell it in any territory where there is need. Concern about "state power," and even about losing control in its own territory if it fails to keep ahead of its obligations, force the company to plan for continued growth.

[8] The validity of extrapolating future demands on the basis of past growth patterns may be questionable. See the discussion in the final sections of this study.

[9] W. P. Allen, Jr., "Future Electric Power Requirements," *Symposium on Water Resource Use and Protection in the Production of Electricity*, October 25, 1968, Ithaca, New York.

Individual utilities such as the NYSE&G plan their construction programs by building well in advance of demands within their territory. They temporarily sell excess firm capacity to other companies until it can be absorbed within their own territory. For example, NYSE&G sales of excess capacity were as follows: 160 megawatts to Pennsylvania Electric; 200 megawatts to Consolidated Edison; and 25 megawatts to Rochester Gas and Electric. Agreements to sell 760 megawatts of firm capacity in 1970 and 1971 have been made with other utilities.[10] Management has claimed that by 1976 the increased capability to be provided by Bell Station will be necessary to meet future growth demands within their own territory. The basis of this calculation is the following: Assuming a continuing 7 per cent annual increase in power demand, the peak load in 1976 would have to be about 2,250 megawatts. By this time the company expects to retire nine of its older, less efficient units totaling about 330 megawatts. To attain the anticipated peak requirement, NYSE&G planning can be briefly summarized: 1,399 megawatts (1968 capacity [11]) plus 640 megawatts (Homer City Plant) plus 830 megawatts (Bell Station) minus 330 megawatts (lost by retiring older units) would yield a generating capability of 2,539 megawatts by 1976.

[10] NYSE&G, *Annual Report*, 1969.

[11] This includes megawatts purchased under firm contract from the New York State Power Authority. At the advantageous rate of 4.82 mills per KW-hr., this contract would be maintained, even if the generating capability were sufficient to meet obligations.

III / *The Actors and the Action*

Plans of the NYSE&G

The NYSE&G decision to locate the Bell nuclear power station on Cayuga Lake was based on several considerations. Cayuga Lake was felt to be particularly desirable primarily because of its year-round cooling capacity. A study of water depths and bridges on access routes indicated that the lake was navigable for shipment of a large reactor vessel, an important factor saving the expense of field fabrication. The location was centrally placed in terms of transmission plans of the utility—in particular, in terms of its ties to other systems. Cayuga Lake was ideally situated halfway between the two main lines of the Northern and Southern EHV transmission grid (see Figure 3, p. 27). Thus a plant on the lake could transmit power conveniently to either line and feed into the exchange system of the New York State Power Pool. Since the new plant would make available more capacity than needed by present NYSE&G customers, the plan was to tie in to the New York State transmission system and sell about 70 per cent of the new capacity the first year.[1]

The utility's decision in June 1967 was greeted enthusiastically by the Tompkins County Board of Supervisors,[2] a governing body of elected county representatives. A prominent member at the time, and chairman of the finance committee, was Harris Dates, county supervisor of Lansing, the home of the projected Bell Station. The Board unanimously voted to invite the company to build its reactor on Cayuga Lake. There was no immediate public reaction, and several individuals who later actively opposed the utility's plans have indicated that their response at the time was a fleeting thought that "progress at last was coming to the area." Early in February 1968, the utility was chosen "Company of the Year" by the Tompkins County Chamber of Commerce, and its president, William A. Lyons, was honored along with Nobel Prize Winner Hans Bethe at an annual Chamber dinner.

The plans were welcomed as an economic boost to the area. Bell Station would employ about six hundred people during the construction phase, and about sixty on a permanent basis. It would contribute significantly to the tax base of the town of Lansing: according to a recent Lansing Planning Board survey, the present full value tax base of about $65.5 million could increase to

[1] *Nucleonics Week*, January 16, 1969.

[2] The Tompkins County Board of Supervisors was changed to the Tompkins County Board of Representatives in January 1970, and Harris Dates became the elected chairman.

between $250 million and $280 million by 1974, if Bell Station were to be built.

Although not all tax revenue would go to the town of Lansing,[3] the increased tax base was expected to lower the tax rate. In addition, the NYSE&G plant fit well with Governor Rockefeller's concern with expanding the power reserve of the State; for the excess capacity would be pooled by tying in with the New York State Power Pool. The Public Service Commission (PSC), responsible for ensuring a wider margin between power demands and available supply, "watched with interest" the increase in production capability through the construction of new generating stations.[4] Bell Station was, in fact, one of six new nuclear plants planned or under construction in New York State in 1968. One plant, the Consolidated Edison Plant at Indian Point, was operating.

Early in July 1967, shortly after the first public announcement of the proposed plant, twenty-five property owners in the area were notified that their property was condemned; for as a public utility, the NYSE&G may exercise the right of eminent domain in

[3] In 1969, the distribution between Lansing and Tompkins County of the tax rate of $10.28 per $1,000 assessment was as follows:

Tompkins County rate	$5.62
Lansing rate	4.65

In addition, the Lansing school-tax rate was $21.48 per $1,000 assessment.

[4] Public Service Commission, *Annual Report* (Albany, 1967), p. xii.

order to expand. Twenty-one accepted the company's offers for sale, but terms could not be reached with four property owners who claimed that the company paid a fair market price for buildings which were then razed and removed from tax rolls, but that land values were held down. The four who refused to sell owned large lots and small summer homes. Feeling the settlement inadequate, they went to litigation, and condemnation procedures were initiated.[5] Eventually, 725 acres were purchased, including 8,000 feet of lake frontage. These activities occurred even before the application for a construction permit was submitted to the AEC.

The utility publicized the details of the station early in 1968. Two workshops were sponsored by the Cayuga Lake Basin Regional Water Resources Planning Board (CLBB) at which representatives from the company presented their plans. The CLBB consists of nonpaid members nominated by the Tompkins County Board of Supervisors and appointed by the State Water Resources Commission. The Board exists under state conservation law to develop a comprehensive water management plan for the region, which it submits to the Water Resources Commission. Its seven members represent local interests in agriculture, industry and commerce, municipal corporations, and public water supply, as well as sports and recreation. It is the only mechanism for intergovernmental cooperation in the lake basin area, and its activities are limited to planning.

[5] Settlements were negotiated out of court.

Utility representatives also talked in February to an informal seminar sponsored by the Water Resources and Marine Sciences Center at Cornell University. The center is an "umbrella" group, with 101 faculty members, many of whom are concerned with water management problems. A study of the Finger Lakes area was one of its four main research thrusts. The seminar, intended as a fact-finding session, was interpreted by some participants as indicating tacit acceptance of the NYSE&G plans. This impression was buttressed by a research prospectus drafted at the Water Resources Center, which appeared to assume the power plant construction was inevitable, and which suggested the unique possibilities it would provide to study thermal pollution. Seneca Lake, as yet unpolluted, was proposed as a control.[6] A research proposal went to the AEC but was turned down. Another proposal, for a study of the

[6] Luther Carter, "Thermal Pollution: A Threat to Cayuga's Waters," *Science*, 162, 3854, November 8, 1968, pp. 118–119. An interesting sidelight suggesting the sensitivity beginning to develop at this time is the correspondence between the Water Resources Center and the editor of *Science*, in reaction to Luther Carter's criticism of the "academic detachment" evident in the center's prospectus. As a rebuttal, the director and associate director of the center submitted a letter and a summary of their testimony at a hearing on November 22, 1968, as evidence that their position was not, in fact, "detached." The editor, however, refused to publish the rebuttal. Carter was called to task by several members of the center for failing to communicate with those he criticized and relying only on the statements of those on one side of a controversial issue.

ecology of the lake, was submitted to the NYSE&G and was accepted; a contract for $135,000 was awarded in June 1968.[7]

The controversy over the NYSE&G plans began to surface with the concern expressed by some participants in the Water Resources Center Seminar. Their first activity in March 1968 was to participate in a two-week series of fifteen-minute broadcasts on an Ithaca radio station, WHCU. Each of these talks included a recorded reassurance from the NYSE&G that they would not damage the lake. It was on the last day of the radio talks that the NYSE&G announced that they had awarded a $300,000 research contract to the Cornell Aeronautical Laboratory to study the physical effects of thermal discharge near Milliken Station.

The extent of the reaction to the Bell Station plans must be considered within the context of the location of the Bell Station site, twelve miles from Cornell University. Here was a varied and highly articulate cluster of scientists and engineers with concerns for the preservation of a major resource in their community. They were willing to use their expertise to enter the confron-

[7] No contract was ever signed, however, due to company stipulations—unacceptable to the university—concerning the biases of employees hired under the contract. The company tried to stipulate that researchers on the project were to be selected only if their nonwork activities suggested they had no biases concerning the issue. They were not, for example, to belong to citizens' groups or similar organizations concerned with environmental issues. The contract remained on an informal basis, accepted by the university research office on the basis of a letter of intent.

tation, and to attempt an evaluation of potential damage to the ecology of the lake. Some of them (water resources engineers, ecologists, fishery biologists, conservationists, and limnologists) were professionally concerned with water resources; others, such as physical scientists, were concerned as citizens, but also had relevant professional expertise to contribute.[8] One of the most active critics of the proposed power station worked on the case every weekend during a three-month period, estimating that at least half his leisure time was devoted to the issue. Another estimated that he spent one month full-time on the case, and subsequently about eight hours a week, on weekends and evenings, for four months.[9] Others were able to relate their work on the lake more directly to their professional research. If the scientific contribution of those volunteering their expertise was calculated on a consulting basis, its cost would be substantial.[10] In addition,

[8] Much of the information concerning scientific activity was obtained through interviews and correspondence with the following scientists and engineers; K. Bingham Cady, Clarence Carlson, Leonard Dworsky, Alfred Eipper, Charles Gates, Alonzo Lawrence, Franklin Moore, Ray Oglesby, and Thomas D. Wright.

[9] An NYSE&G spokesman noted critically that he had encountered difficulty in getting scientists to invest their time in community or charitable activities.

[10] Consulting fees vary from about $75 to several hundred dollars per day, depending on whether one is consulting for government or private industry. Assuming a fee of $100 per day, eight hours of work a week for four months, plus a month full-time, would cost about $4,300 for the time of just one man.

political and organizational activity, preparation of testimony, and dissemination of information required a great investment of time. Without this voluntary activity, it is doubtful that the controversy would have developed.

Scientific Activity

Evaluating the possibility of ecological damage to the lake required the cooperation of scientists from many disciplines, and several interdisciplinary groups were brought together. The first of these was organized by Professor Alfred Eipper, an ecologist specializing in fishery biology in the Department of Conservation at Cornell. His interest in the issue was stimulated by a course he had been teaching in water resources management. Disturbed by the possibilities of thermal pollution of the lake, in March he called together a group of his colleagues who he felt might share his concerns. About twenty people came to the meeting. From Eipper's point of view as an ecologist, a position had to be taken on the utility's plans before irreversible damage to the lake occurred. It was agreed that a position paper would be developed, summarizing the existing state of knowledge concerning the thermal properties of the lake.

Eipper wrote the initial draft, circulated it within the University and elsewhere, and received extensive comments and criticism. The report, considerably revised after circulation through four drafts, appeared on May 27, 1968.[11] It was signed by seventeen contributors from

[11] Alfred W. Eipper *et al.*, *Thermal Pollution of Cayuga Lake by a Proposed Power Plant* (Ithaca, New York, 1968).

several disciplines including conservation, limnology, biology, botany, geology, and engineering.[12] A preface noted that the paper, reflecting the knowledge of its authors, had "resulted from the conviction that . . . professionals should contribute to public decisions on the management of natural resources." The Eipper report summarized known effects and raised several questions on possible effects of a heat discharge on the thermal and nutrient structure of the lake, and its likely implications for the aquatic environment.

The report predicted, on the basis of other studies, that as the normal stratification pattern is upset through the pumping of water from the hypolimnion, the natural eutrophication process would be augmented. Eutrophication is a process normally occurring when nutrients such as nitrates and phosphates drain into lakes from the surrounding watershed and increase lake fertility. The report claimed it to be a virtually irreversible

[12] Dean Arnold (limnology); Wayne T. Bell, Jr. (conservation); Clifford Berg (limnology); Clarence A. Carlson, Jr. (fishery biology); Norman C. Dondero (applied microbiology); John L. Forney (fishery biology); David M. Green, Jr. (conservation); Lawrence S. Hamilton (conservation); John M. Kingsbury (botany); Alonzo W. Lawrence (water resources engineering); Simpson Linke (electrical engineering); Hugh F. Mulligan (Aquatic Studies); Gerald J. Paulik (fishery biology); Carl L. Schofield, Jr. (conservation); John W. Wells (geology); Bruce T. Wilkins (conservation); Alfred W. Eipper (fishery biology), chairman. About eight of these seventeen signatories made an extensive contribution; others made minor changes. In signing, the seventeen authors indicated both their participation and their agreement with the contents.

process, accelerated by lakeside development of housing, agriculture, and industry, whereby biological production can eventually cause a lake to choke with algae and weed growth.[13] Biological productivity would be stimulated in two ways. The continuous addition of heated water would delay the cooling and mixing of the lake in the fall, extending the stratification period and consequently the biological growing season. Moreover, drawing the available nutrients from the hypolimnion and discharging them into the warmer waters of the epilimnion would increase biological productivity. At the same time, the oxygen available for animal life in the hypolimnion would be depleted, affecting the food sources of fish. The Eipper report described the effects of eutrophication in other lakes, such as Lake Erie, pointing out the "pea soup" appearance caused by the proliferation of algae.[14]

To minimize eutrophication, the report recommended alternative methods of cooling the discharged water, either through the use of cooling towers or of cooling ponds (this latter method requiring an area of at least

[13] The question of irreversibility of the eutrophication process is a controversial one in siting controversies, and will be discussed later (pp. 95 ff.).

[14] The phrase "pea soup" was to be picked up by journalists, and served later as one basis for criticism of this report as emotionally biased and misleading. For a study of eutrophication in New York State water resources, see D. N. Hamilton and J. P. Barlow, *Eutrophication of Water Resources of New York State*, Cornell University Water Resources Center, publication 4, November 1966.

two square miles).[15] The report concluded that although the increase in biological production, and therefore of eutrophication, was unpredictable, the practical impossibility of reversing damage imposed the need for cautious consideration of all alternatives.

When the report was distributed for revision, four of those initially involved in the early meetings of the Eipper Committee refused to sign, considering it to represent an inappropriate scientific stance. In fact, the Eipper report, highly influential in generating political activity, soon became a source of strain within the scientific community.

This strain reflected not so much substantive disagreement as concern with the mode of presentation of scientific data, the appropriate behavior of scientists with respect to public issues, and the effect of publicity on the scientific dimensions of the problem. At one extreme were those who felt that the "credibility of science was threatened by scientists who took a position on an issue. At the other were those who felt that taking a firm position was necessary. Disagreements were subtle and alliances shifting; concern for the lake brought individuals together on specific problems. Strain persisted, however, reinforced by the public pressure to take a position and the inconclusiveness of the evidence available on the ecology of the lake.

Uncertainty concerning the effects of the power sta-

[15] The report's discussion of alternative cooling systems is somewhat confusing. For a discussion of relevant possibilities, see pp. 68–69 of this study.

tion became increasingly apparent as new groups formed to study technical aspects of the problem. In August 1968, Clarence A. Carlson, a fishery biologist from the Cornell Department of Conservation, brought together a group of twelve scientists representing the disciplines of medicine, limnology, ecology, conservation, physical biology, and physics, to study the radiological hazards of the Bell Station. The group included five persons who were on the Eipper committee.[16] Their report,[17] appearing in December, was intended to "permit a better-informed decision as to whether the public benefits from the proposed station outweigh its liabilities."

The Carlson report was drafted by Carlson and circulated for revisions in the same manner as the Eipper report. Its position was that accidents were unlikely, though not outside the realm of possibility. They were very concerned, however, about radiological wastes produced in the course of normal daily operation. These wastes have their source in small quantities of radionuclides added to the primary coolant by neutron acti-

[16] Dean E. Abrahamson (University of Minnesota Medical School—medicine); Dean E. Arnold (limnology); LaMont Cole (ecology); Alfred Eipper (fishery biology); Lawrence S. Hamilton (conservation); Jay F. Kirkpatrick (physical biology and physiology; Gene E. Likens (limnology); Jay Orear (physics); Robert O. Pohl (physics); Carl L. Schofield, Jr. (conservation); Robert H. Whittaker (ecology); Clarence A. Carlson, Jr. (fishery biology), chairman. Six contributors did not sign the document.

[17] Clarence A. Carlson *et al., Radioactivity and a Proposed Power Plant on Cayuga Lake* (Ithaca, New York, November 22, 1968).

vation of corrosion products, leakage of fission products, and production of tritium. Some low radiation level wastes would be routinely released into the condenser cooling water and into the lake. While the company's estimates of the quantity of radionuclides to be released were well below AEC maxima, the report argued that "localized concentration of radionuclides by currents, eddies, or wave action, is a likely possibility. After a few years of plant operation, and accumulation of radionuclides, these processes could result in local concentrations in excess of maximum permissible concentrations." [18] Moreover, the report argued, plants and animals may concentrate radionuclides which, through a food chain, could unpredictably affect other aquatic organisms. The report recommended that, in view of the difficulty of accurately predicting radionuclide concentrations and their possible effects on the lake ecology, the AEC tighten its requirements in this case, and state agencies consider radiological as well as thermal issues. It also urged a design modification which would virtually eliminate radionuclide discharge at an additional $500,000 in construction costs and about $100,000 in annual operating costs.

The Engineering College at Cornell also undertook a study during the summer of 1968.[19] A committee

[18] AEC rules, however, do require radiation accumulation to be considered.

[19] Franklin K. Moore *et al.*, *Engineering Aspects of Thermal Discharges to a Stratified Lake* (College of Engineering, Cornell University, Ithaca, New York, 1969).

headed by Franklin K. Moore, Chairman of the Thermal Engineering Department, was appointed and supported by the Engineering College. The group included six engineers from water resources engineering, environmental systems engineering, aerospace engineering, mechanical engineering, thermal engineering, and applied physics.[20] They met weekly during the summer of 1968, then each participant wrote on his facet of the problem. The report, appearing in February 1969, was compiled and edited by Moore on the basis of complete drafts submitted by each participant. It was signed as a single document by all participants.

The report was a theoretical analysis which focused on the physical consequences of the heat transfer underlying biological and ecological questions. It emphasized a consideration of the total parameters of the lake, taking issue with NYSE&G-supported research, which focused only on the area near the site. Measurement programs, it claimed, should be undertaken not only near the plume created by the discharge but over the entire lake. The report first dealt with transport processes, or turbulence caused by winds, flushing, and discharge, estimating that the effect of forced mixing through pumping could cause a 10 per cent increase in the vertical exchange of nutrients during the stratified summer

[20] W. H. Brutsaert (water resources engineering); K. B. Cady (applied physics); C. S. ReVelle (environmental systems engineering); A. R. Seebass (aerospace engineering); D. G. Shepherd (mechanical engineering); F. K. Moore (thermal engineering), chairman.

months. The report also considered the heat balance of the lake, estimating that the discharge from the plant would represent 7 per cent of the direct heat received by the lake from the sun, "a neither overwhelming nor negligible perturbation." [21]

It is interesting that in public hearings in November 1968, Stern Lyon, a system results engineer in the NYSE&G, took issue with this estimate of 7 per cent, despite the fact that it was based on measurements of average solar energy actually absorbed by the lake. Lyon misinterpreted the calculation and figured a higher amount of total radiant energy based on an hourly comparison only. Thus, he calculated that the addition of the heat from the power plant would be from one per cent to four per cent, a much less significant perturbation than 7 per cent.

The Moore report calculated that the increase in the yearly average surface temperature would be 0.9° F.,[22] a temperature rise which would be shared by the hypolimnion to a degree depending on presently unknown characteristics of the stratification process. In the absence of a theoretical basis on which to base prediction of the stratification process, the report urged an increase in thermal efficiency and conservative thermal pollution standards.

[21] Moore, *op. cit.*, p. 23.

[22] This assumed 100 per cent utilization of the plant capacity. A realistic utilization of 80 per cent would bring the temperature rise down to 0.7° F. in agreement with a study done under NYSE&G contract by Cornell Aeronautical Laboratory (see pp. 51 ff.).

Most of the scientific activity stimulated by the Eipper report was focused on the possible effect of the power plant on the nearby part of the lake. But several persons considered this approach too limited, and proposed the development of a strategy which considered the lake as a whole. One of these, K. Bingham Cady, a participant in the Moore study, raised the question of the temperature and distance standards for heated water discharges proposed, but not yet established, by the State Department of Health. On October 2, 1968, Cady drafted a letter to the Department of Health, which was, at the time, struggling with the issue of thermal criteria. The letter proposed criteria for a lake standard based on the effects of heated water on the ecology of the lake as a whole, rather than near the point of discharge. This contrasted with the health department's intended temperature-distance standards, which would limit the surface increase beyond a specified distance from the plume, or discharge point. The letter, signed by Cady, Franklin Moore, Alfred Eipper, Clarence Carlson, and John Barlow, was intended to be a compromise which might be agreeable to the company, since it recognized that "if the heated water is floated onto the surface of the lake, a larger fraction of the heat is dissipated directly to the atmosphere." [23] This would prevent mixing heat into the lake and at the same time would permit discharge of a heated plume on the surface. It appeared to be a reasonable suggestion in terms of the ecologi-

[23] Letter from K. Bingham Cady *et al.* to Dwight Metzler, New York State Department of Health, October 2, 1968.

cal concerns of conservationists, and one which the NYSE&G could endorse, since it would not require a change in their plans. In fact, on April 11, 1969, when William A. Lyons, president of the NYSE&G, announced postponement of Bell Station to the company's Board of Directors, he said: "We have been hopeful that the great volume of research which we have sponsored would demonstrate with reasonable certainty that we could discharge the heated water from our plant on the surface of the lake in a way that would effectively and economically provide thermal protection for Cayuga Lake." [24] Even in March 1969, at the Water Resources Commission hearings on the proposed standards, company engineers were in some agreement with Cady with respect to the proposed standards. At the time of Cady's proposal, however, when a company engineer was asked to sign Cady's letter he declined; and, as we shall see, the compromise proposal was to have no effect whatsoever on health department regulations.

In October 1968, at the same time that Cady was proposing a broader perspective on the question of thermal criteria, a physicist, James A. Krumhansl, proposed a broader research strategy suggesting an interesting approach to the technical problem which had been overlooked in other reports. Both Eipper's report and the NYSE&G-sponsored research restricted their concern to the damage that might result from the pumping and thermal effect of the power station. In contrast, Krum-

[24] William A. Lyons, statement to the NYSE&G Board of Directors, April 11, 1969.

hansl assumed that the lake ecology was already damaged due to a variety of pollution sources such as sewage and agriculture, and asked: "Is it possible to use a major energy source to *beneficiate* the lake, i.e. in some sense to combat these forces (chemical, biological, etc.) which are now driving it?" [25] He proposed to use the plant as an energy source to cool the epilimnion by circulating a volume of cold water from the hypolimnion. He calculated that a normal increase of 50 per cent of the water pumped through condensers for cooling purposes would be sufficient to cool the epilimnion by about 10° F. This process, less costly than cooling towers, would have a positive effect on the lake by decreasing biological activity and reversing, in part, the existing state of eutrophication.

Krumhansl's proposal led to a series of meetings out of which developed several suggestions for dealing with overall lake problems. Professors Donald Belcher (civil engineering) and Simpson Linke (electrical engineering) proposed a pumped-water storage facility and calculated that the costs would be comparable to cooling towers. In discussion of these and other schemes, it became apparent that the thermal problem was far from intractable; the main problem would be circulation of nutrients. In this respect, the pumped-water scheme would have the added benefit of removing nutrient-laden water from the lake. Belcher suggested that a joint

[25] J. A. Krumhansl, *Ideas for Discussion of "Thermal Pollution" and Cayuga Lake Protection or Beneficiation,* October 1, 1968 (mimeographed).

effort by the NYSE&G and the community to seek state support for such a facility might resolve the thermal pollution problem in a way that would have positive implications for the lake.

Early in 1969, Belcher, Linke, and Eipper met with two NYSE&G representatives, Gordon Black, manager of the Ithaca area, and Robert Hobart, an engineer who was slated to become the superintendent of the proposed Bell Station. After initial discussions, technical material concerning the pumped-water storage facilities was presented to the two NYSE&G representatives, to indicate the possibilities of the proposal and to lay the basis for further discussion. No public disclosure of these data was made, since the computations were based on rough, nonoptimized estimates of the possibilities of the proposed cooling-pond site. However, NYSE&G engineers calculated on the basis of these estimates that the cost of the proposed pumped-storage system would be about five times the acceptable figure. The issue was raised during a public discussion in February 1969, when Mr. Albert D. Tuttle, vice president and chief engineer of the NYSE&G, presented these cost estimates. Although Belcher and Linke both protested that the NYSE&G, figures were based on their very rough estimates, it was gradually agreed that the scheme was likely to be expensive, and the subject was referred back to Belcher and Linke for further study.[26]

[26] The above material is from letters in the *Ithaca Journal*, December 11 and 18, 1968, and personal communication with Simpson Linke.

Eipper participated in these discussions, but did not incorporate any of the proposals into his public statements; nor did he modify his references to thermal pollution. The suggestions were never seriously considered in subsequent discussion of alternatives. More accurate cost estimates on these proposals would require extensive engineering surveys. Such studies have not been undertaken to date. Further detailed studies by the NYSE&G, CAL, and the Moore research group, concentrated on the more restricted problem of disturbing the lake minimally. The main conclusions of these studies do not seem to conflict with the Linke-Belcher proposal and the data on which their work was based.

While these activities were taking place, the NYSE&G contracted its own research at a cost of about $500,000. Two major contracts were awarded. One was for about $320,000 to the Cornell Aeronautical Labortaory (CAL) in Buffalo, an independent research contract organization owned by Cornell University.[27] This contract was to study the physical effects of thermal discharge near the present fossil fuel station. The other contract was for $135,000 to the Cornell Water Resources Center to study ecological effects (see above, p. 38). In addition, a small contract was given to John Storr, a long-time utility consultant at the University of Buffalo.

The CAL engineers took an empirical approach and focused on the area of the lake near the existing Milliken

[27] The bill to the company was more than this, due to unforeseen contingencies including reported vandalism of equipment.

Station, studying the plume created by the discharge and its effect on the surface. Three types of data formed the basis of a report which appeared in November 1969.[28] First, aerial measurements were taken of surface temperature profiles, using infra-red scanning devices. Second, the vertical structure of the lake was monitored from nine stations, within three thousand feet of the site, measuring for the diffusion and heat exchange caused by the existing power station. Finally, meterological measurements were used to evaluate the effects of weather conditions on the rate at which the higher temperature of the plume decays. The conclusions, consistent with those of the Moore report, were that thermal impact of the proposed station would cause an overall increase in the temperature of the surface of 0.7° F., or less than 10 per cent of the normal fluctuation. The mechanical transfer of cooling water from the hypolimnion would increase the volume of the epilimnion during the stratification period which would be lengthened, at most, by four to five days at each end. This was of the same order as a natural fluctuation. The increase in the maximum heat content of the lake would be about 2 per cent of the annual heat budget. The changes, vis-à-vis normal fluctuations, are summarized in Table 6.

Thus, the CAL report suggested that the effects would be of the same order or less than normal fluctuations, though always unidirectional. It noted, however,

[28] Cornell Aeronautical Laboratory, *Cayuga Lake and Bell Station Technical Reports* VT 2616-0-3/VT 2616-0-2/VT 2616-0-1, November, 1969.

that coming to firm conclusions requires many more actual observations, and a greater understanding of the complexity of factors affecting turbulence. The report was completed in November 1969, and, at the time of this writing, was under review by the NYSE&G.

Research supported by the NYSE&G also was under way during the summer of 1968 at the Cornell Water Resources Center. A group of seven scientists interested in working on the study was formed, headed by a re-

Table 6. Changes in temperature and stratification period of Cayuga Lake

	Present	Normal fluctuation	Bell Station effect
Maximum surface temperature (August)	72° F.	±5°	+0.8°
Minimum surface temperature (March)	36° F.	±4°	+0.6°
Stratification period (days)	170–200	±15	+10

source economist, David Allee, and an ecologist, Ray Oglesby.[29] The group came together under constrained circumstances. Several individuals, experts in relevant scientific fields, were logical choices, but their known concern with environmental problems precluded their participation. The utility requested that no one who

[29] David Allee (agricultural economics) and Ray T. Oglesby (aquatic science), editors; John P. Barlow (oceanography); Charles D. Gates (civil engineering); John C. Thompson (physical biology), Thomas D. Wright (conservation); William D. Youngs (conservation).

was likely to have already formed an opinion should work on the project. Thus a man outside Cornell, Thomas D. Wright, was brought in as a research associate in the Department of Conservation for the study; he was to be the author of fourteen of the twenty chapters in the final report. Bringing in an outsider posed particular problems of coordination and control in an interdisciplinary study. Moreover, Wright soon became a source of controversy when he joined the Citizens Committee to Save Cayuga Lake (CSCL). Because Wright left Cornell after completing his research, the major editing and summarizing was done by Ray Oglesby, also a newcomer to Cornell, who joined the faculty in October 1968, well after the NYSE&G study was under way. Thus the constraints imposed by the utility's concern with objectivity led to additional problems of research organization.

The work of this group dealt basically with the same subject as the Eipper report, but its intention differed considerably. The work plan of the study, formulated in May 1968, indicated that "the group would *not* attempt to comment upon the broader questions of public policy involved. Administrative, economic, political, or psychological questions would be put aside in order to objectively evaluate the physical, chemical, and biological impacts of heat addition to a water body." [30] Data

[30] Ray T. Oglesby and David J. Allee (eds.), *Ecology of Cayuga Lake and the Proposed Bell Station*, Publication 27, Water Resources and Marine Sciences Center, Ithaca, New York, September 1969, Introduction.

were collected in order to provide a base-line evaluation of the lake. The report was issued in September 1969 and contained twenty studies, as well as conclusions and recommendations. The articles were individually signed; thus each writer was responsible for his own statements.

The actual data collection, terminating in April 1969, was closely observed by NYSE&G engineers who met regularly with the group and participated in discussions. Their presence was described as being sometimes useful and sometimes irritating. It was emphasized, however, that this did not interfere with the results of the study; and, sensitive to possible criticism concerning the source of support, the group insisted that the results be published without company editing.

The report began by interpreting historical data on the lake, indicating that it may just be entering a eutrophication stage. The study sampled from seven stations at various times during the season to establish base-line information for biochemical and radionuclide studies. Material was compiled on oxygen distribution, on alkalinity and pH, on heat budget and water temperature, on currents, on the hydrology of the lake, and on phytoplankton and plant nutrients. The results were presented with caveats as to the difficulty of drawing quantitative conclusions. It was estimated that at the time of greatest thermal effect algae could increase by 5 per cent. There could be a net seasonal decrease in the oxygen in the hypolimnion; but such changes were interpreted as insignificant. The effect of increased temperature and a longer stratification season were also predicted to be insignificant for the lake as a whole. The report stressed the uncertainty of knowledge in this area and suggested additional studies. It concluded that "limnologists know so little about the ecological significance of some of these environmental parameters, that prediction of biological effects would be highly conjectural even if exact descriptions of the physical changes were available." [31] Despite problems, the study did make publicly available a sizable body of empirical data about the lake.

During this period of research, the NYSE&G proceeded with its plan, applying for an AEC construction permit in March 1968, and beginning site clearance next to Milliken Station in April.[32] Excavation of 15 million cubic feet of shale was completed and concrete forms installed before the winter, at a cost of about one million dollars in addition to the $700,000 purchase price of the land. Engineering development was contracted to United Engineers and Constructors, Inc., a Boston and Philadelphia concern, which attached 120 of their employees to this project. By September, however, it became evident to the utility that it would have to contend not only with ambiguous standards of thermal pollution and with conservationist criticism, but also with an aroused community.

[31] *Ibid.*, p. 452.

[32] Excavation is legally permissible, without a permit, to the point of pouring concrete. However, concrete capping of the excavation was permitted at the site to prevent erosion.

Citizen Activity and NYSE&G Response

The Cayuga Lake Preservation Association (CLPA) was the most likely of existing organizations to become involved in the issue. The CLPA was formed in 1956 to deal with sewage problems in the lake drainage area, and by 1968 it included some 350 lakeshore property owners as members. On July 15, 1968, in response to the Eipper report, the CLPA issued a statement urging that, in the light of disagreement among scientists on the effect of nuclear power plants, the company delay construction until definitive answers were obtained regarding potential damage to the lake environment. It also urged the incorporation of an alternative cooling system as recommended by the Eipper report. The CLPA was divided, however, on the issue of becoming directly involved in the fight to support its position, in part because of its recent heavy involvement in a controversial campaign in which it opposed fluoridation.

On August 15, Eipper called a community meeting in Ithaca for concerned citizens. Thirty people attended. As a result of this meeting, David D. Comey, a research associate in Soviet Studies at Cornell and director of a private research institute on Soviet science, offered to form a citizens' organization, the Citizens Committee to Save Cayuga Lake (CSCL). In just a few weeks officers were elected, a press release issued, and a board of sponsors selected. The thirty-three members of this board were respected and well-established members of the community, active in other civic organizations. Professional men were relatively dominant in the heterogeneous group, which included persons affiliated with universities in the lake region, four local political figures, four attorneys, four physicians, a city planner, a newspaper publisher and former Commissioner of Construction of New York, a stock broker, and several insurance and real estate brokers. All the bank presidents in Ithaca were approached but, anticipating the goals of the organization as potentially conflicting with their economic interest, none would consider affiliation.

The organization's official purpose was "to inform citizens of the Cayuga Lake region about potential sources of bacterial, chemical, thermal and radioactive pollution of the lake, and to coordinate the efforts of all concerned organizations and individuals to prevent and eradicate any pollution endangering the foremost natural resource of the region." [33] Its position, stressed at every public hearing and in the press,[34] was not one of opposition to nuclear power; rather, the emphasis was on the present design of the plant, which, it was felt, afforded inadequate environmental protection. Attention was also directed to inadequacies in the system of regulation and the standards by which resources were protected.

The Executive Director, Comey, was highly skillful,

[33] Information concerning the organization is available in David D. Comey (ed.), *Cayuga Lake Handbook* (The Citizens Committee to Save Cayuga Lake: Ithaca, New York, 1969), pp. 102–105. This volume also contains transcripts of hearings, clippings, and miscellany relating to the controversy.

[34] *New York Times*, September 22, 1968.

and the CSCL was successful in its goal of coordinating the efforts of those concerned with the issue. Sixty people attended its organizational meeting in September 1968, and within several months the organization boasted three hundred members plus several thousand other persons associated through their membership in various organizations which affiliated with the CSCL.[35] These included local sportsmen's groups, the CLPA, the Seneca Lake Waterways Association, and the Lake Champlain Committee, a group which faced a similar threat and hoped to gain experience from the CSCL. By September 1969, the paid membership had grown to 854 and $16,323 had been raised from dues and contributions.

The CSCL sought and received wide publicity. It reprinted and distributed more than 22,000 copies of the Eipper and Carlson reports. Newspaper coverage also helped to arouse citizens' interest. In 1968 and 1969 the *Ithaca Journal*, with a circulation of 18,900, printed about seventy-five unsigned and forty signed articles relating specifically to the case. Newspapers from surrounding communities on the lake also commented on the issue, and headlines such as "Cayuga Lake Shouldn't Look Like Diluted 'Pea Soup' "[36] served to foster public concern.

The CSCL structure (see Chart 1) was described by

[35] Membership dues are $5.00. Associate members are affiliated through their membership in associated organizations. In addition, there is a category of paid associate membership of $2.00 available for students.

[36] *Auburn Citizen Advertiser*, August 8, 1968.

Comey as informal, flexible, and democratic, yet highly centralized. Participation by all was welcomed and all activities were public. Open meetings took place monthly throughout the fall of 1968 and early spring of 1969 and were attended by NYSE&G representatives. Some of the meetings attracted nearly two hundred people. Speakers included NYSE&G and General Electric representatives, and experts on thermal and radiological factors and on legislative and regulatory problems.

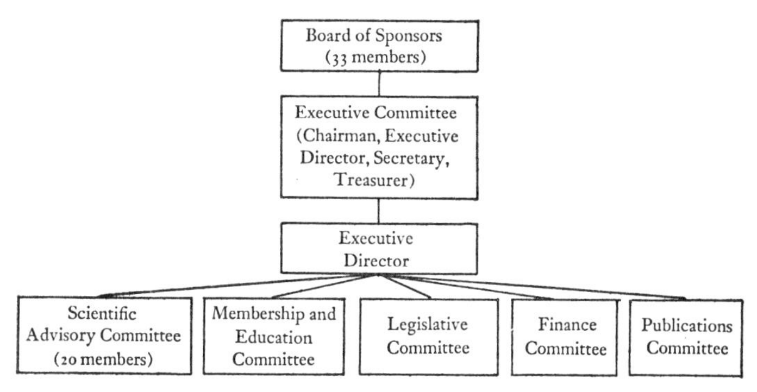

Chart 1. Organizational structure of the Citizens Committee to Save Cayuga Lake (CSCL)

The core of the CSCL is a science advisory committee, a group of twenty scientists, including Eipper and Carlson, who work closely with the Director and participate in all CSCL activities. All members volunteer their time. The Director estimates this was worth from $50,000 to $100,000 during the first active year of the organization. By the end of 1969, $9,485 was spent by the organization, largely on publications, materials, and some transportation costs. Only $937 was spent on legal fees, since the CSCL made only "limited appearance" at hearings at this time. At a meeting in January 1969, however, the two hundred members present were polled, and all but one supported a plan for the organization to appear as an intervening party should there be an AEC hearing on the power plant. This would be an expensive move, requiring legal counsel, and Harold Green of George Washington University, a well-known atomic energy attorney, has been retained to represent the group.

The autonomy of the Executive Director gives the CSCL a flexibility crucial to its aggressive strategy. He can transact most of the organization's business without consulting the membership, a fact which gave the CSCL tactical advantage in the controversy. Press releases, needing no approval, were turned out in a matter of hours. Prompt and open responses were made to public inquiries. In contrast, the NYSE&G was slow to release information, was most often inaccessible to the press, and was cautious if not defensive regarding public controversy. "The company is not in the business of answering questions from the public." [37]

Although slow to respond to controversy, the utility did establish a Bell Station information program "to

[37] Quoted in a letter from Dean E. Arnold to the NYSE&G Ithaca Area manager. The NYSE&G claims that Mr. Arnold was later called by the company in an effort to arrange a meeting so that his views on the proposed plant could be explored, but Mr. Arnold refused to attend such a meeting.

provide the public with an ongoing report of the Corporation's activities regarding the proposed nuclear plant." Between March 1967 and June 1969 the information service issued twenty-seven news releases and provided company representatives for 112 speeches before local clubs. Eighty community representatives were flown by the company to the Connecticut Yankee Atomic Power Plant for a demonstration tour of a nuclear plant. Public meetings and presentations were given to community leaders, planning and water management boards, and representatives from state and federal agencies.

The utility's strongest argument was the potential economic impact of Bell Station. At a meeting of two hundred businessmen and government and labor representatives in February 1969, it gained substantial local support. The president of the Building Trades Council, impressed with the estimated construction payroll of twenty-five million dollars, said: "We don't have the fears that some people have about this." And Mayor Jack Kiely of Ithaca said: "I don't see anything that should stop the building of the plant. Actually, most everyone is for it and is convinced it will not be harmful. I'm for it 100%." [38]

But most of the company's presentations and releases tended to be defensive, and sought to reassure the public without refuting specific criticisms. The NYSE&G never joined issue with its critics except on certain questions

[38] *Journal Courier*, February 20, 1969 (reprint from *Binghamton Press*).

of radiological waste raised by the Carlson report. There was little substantive response to the pollution charge. The defensiveness was rooted in the feeling that, as the accused party, they could not win the debate in direct confrontation with their critics. They saw their position as resting on their "credibility," that is, on the good will accumulated through past customer relationships; nothing they could say would persuade people to believe they would not damage the lake. From the company's point of view, their opponents, being accusers with a critical posture and emotional bias, could use indiscriminate evidence because they had little to lose.[39]

This defensive attitude was evident on several occasions. For example, on October 25, 1968, the environmental effects of nuclear power stations were discussed at a meeting of the Oswego Basin Regional Water Resources Board. Papers were read by speakers from several utilities including the NYSE&G and state agencies on power needs, siting requirements, and research programs. The papers pointed out that utilities operated with awareness of environmental problems and were, in fact, taking the lead in developing relevant technologies. It was asserted that increased power generation in no way conflicted with the need for conservation.[40]

In response to various attacks, the NYSE&G manage-

[39] From the point of view of the CSCL Director, the *only* basis of influence and credibility of the CSCL was the validity of the data they presented. Critics, he claimed, can afford to make no mistakes.

[40] *Symposium on Water Resource Use and Protection in the Production of Electricity*, Ithaca, New York, October 25, 1968.

ment's main position was that the charges were "premature," based on conditions not yet definitively established. They repeatedly pointed to the extensive research under way as evidence of their intention to be "a good citizen operating in the public interest." [41] This argument was not good copy and only about one quarter of the press coverage on the controversy focused on the NYSE&G position; this was largely in press releases and interviews. While all CSCL meetings were covered —suggesting the Director's close relationship with the press—few of the Bell Station information program activities received attention. Thus, the NYSE&G position was less clearly stated than that of the CSCL, while the continual flow of publicity from the latter served to keep the company off balance and public opinion active.

The success of the CSCL is reflected in the fact that it became a focus for local activity in various townships on the lake. Traditionally, there is little cooperation between townships. Each municipality is empowered to manage its own waste water disposal and water supply program. There has been no coordination of these and other programs or land use practices which are relevant to the lake. On this issue, however, resolutions that the plant should not be built if the lake were to be harmed were passed by several town boards and mailed to the CSCL as evidence of support. For example, the Board of Trustees of the Village of Union Springs resolved that the plant should not be built "until the CSCL, Al-

[41] *Ithaca Journal*, September 11, 1969.

fred W. Eipper and David D. Comey and other persons and organizations making claims against said NYSE&G be fully and adequately controverted and refuted . . . so that no nuclear pollution of said lake is to be anticipated from the construction and operation of said power plant." [42]

The CSCL used other tactics, appearing at relevant hearings, establishing contacts and legal support, and generally working to delay construction, on the theory that the expense of delay constituted pressure.[43] The Executive Director estimated, on the basis of experience in other controversies, that delays in the granting of an operating license could cost the utility about $100,000 per day.

Public Hearings and Political Activity

The Bell Station controversy was first brought up at a public hearing in April 1968, when an exchange of letters between concerned citizens of Ithaca and NYSE&G engineers was mailed to Edmund S. Muskie, chairman of the Senate Subcommittee on Air and Water Pollution of the Committee on Public Works. The letters appeared as evidence in the subcommittee's hearing concerning the extent to which environmental fac-

[42] Passed unanimously, December 18, 1969.

[43] In November 1968 the company's expenditures were reported at hearings as about $2 million, but their annual report for 1968 indicates that $4.2 million had been expended for engineering, land, site preparation, and research. At this time, $22 million was budgeted for Bell Station for 1969. By the end of 1969 more than $10 million had been spent.

tors were considered in the selection of power plant sites.

In September 1968, the case was brought up again in another context. At a hearing of the Joint Legislative Committee on Consumer Protection, Assemblywoman Constance Cook (Republican, New York) stated that an interdepartmental agency could more appropriately control atomic power development than the present uncoordinated system of state jurisdiction. She noted that site clearance expenses, incurred by the utility on the gamble that a permit would be granted, could be charged to the public as a part of operating costs, and suggested that the Public Service Law was inadequate to control rates in such a case.

Public hearings specifically related to the Cayuga Lake case were held in Ithaca on November 22, 1968, by the state Joint Legislative Committee on Conservation, Natural Resources, and Scenic Beauty, chaired by Assemblyman Charles Stockmeister. In the climate of contention which prevailed by this time, several groups spoke for postponing the building of Bell Station until further evidence concerning possible damage could be accumulated, and urged design changes to ensure minimal damage. These groups included the CLPA, the Tompkins County Chamber of Commerce, the New York State Conservation Council, the League of Women Voters, the Finger Lakes Chapter of the Sierra Club, and the Seneca Lake Waterways Association. The Cayuga Lake Basin Regional Water Resources Planning Board (CLBB) did not take an active position, but placed on the utility the "burden of proof" that it would not damage the lake.[44] Several persons and groups, however, indicated their reluctance to postpone the construction. Lansing Supervisor Harris Dates, thinking of tax benefits to Lansing Township, supported the utility. Representatives of the Building Trades Council and the Builders' Exchange considered the benefits to the construction industry, and the Ithaca Taxpayers' Association said, "For once in our history let's try to get something on the local tax roll and not off it." [45]

The CSCL took the most active role at the hearings, but maintained a strategically moderate position. Its Director stressed that the organization was not opposed to construction of the station, and concerned himself with design alternatives to minimize thermal and radiological pollution. He presented at the hearings information concerning alternative cooling arrangements to the intended NYSE&G system of direct discharge of water from the condenser into the lake It would be technically possible to construct a cooling pond with a large surface area (about three to four square miles for a 1,000-MWe unit) in which discharged water would be cooled through conduction and evaporation. Three kinds of cooling towers were possible. The system proposed for Bell Station was a natural draft cooling system in which discharged water is pumped into large, hyperbolic towers and cooled by contact with air. Water not lost through evaporation is recirculated. Another system uses mechanical draft cooling towers which have

[44] *Ithaca Journal*, November 22, 1968.
[45] *Ibid.*, November 23, 1968.

fans to circulate air through the water. These require smaller chimneys than the natural draft system, but the cost is high. Finally, a dry tower system has water circulated through a radiator with an enormous heat transfer surface. Air blown over the radiators cools the water with no loss by evaporation. This is an expensive system, but useful in arid regions.

At the Stockmeister hearings the CSCL also recommended that the state create definitive standards immediately relevant to the siting of power stations on thermally stratified lakes, and that it strengthen its control over the construction of nuclear units. Two petitions were presented which were later to go to the state legislature. One recommended a more active role for the Department of Conservation in the licensing process; the other requested the establishment of basic criteria against which to evaluate thermal and radiological pollution.

Most of the testimony at the Stockmeister hearings was sympathetic to the CSCL position. For example, two directors of the Water Resources Center who were earlier criticized for "scientific detachment" testified, establishing their concern over the lack of effective administrative arrangements to resolve such issues as the Bell Station case. They recommended that, in the absence of adequate knowledge, all available technology be utilized to eliminate deterioration of the lake.

Local political leaders also assumed a position sympathetic to the CSCL. State Senator Thomas Day (Republican) from Seneca County, and Assemblywoman Constance Cook (Republican) from Tompkins County were on the board of sponsors of the CSCL. U.S. Congressman Samuel Stratton (Democrat) flew to Ithaca for the hearings to support the CSCL position. Others who indicated support were former State Senator George Metcalf, Paul O'Dwyer, Democratic candidate for United States Senator in 1968, and Melvin Hazard, the Democratic candidate for the Tompkins-Tioga County Assembly seat.

Congressman Howard Robison (Republican) expressed sympathy, at the time, with the citizens' committee; but by March 5, 1969, in statements to the Subcommittee on Air and Water Pollution of the Senate Committee on Public Works, he had clearly changed his position. In a discussion of broad national issues raised by power plant disputes, he urged that regulatory agencies avoid putting special burdens on nuclear-fueled plants. At the same time, he stated that he had resisted taking sides on the local level: "I do regret the aura of suspicion that has come to surround the NYSE&G effort to move forward with this project in the minds of some of my constituents . . . NYSE&G has for many years been a 'good neighbor' to those of us who have been its customers, and we are all indebted to it for its willingness to make the investment represented by the Cayuga Lake plant in an effort to meet our own future demands. . . . All of us want progress." [46]

At the hearings, politicians attacked the administrative adequacy of existing regulatory agencies and the extent to which conflicting pressures are brought to bear on licensing procedures as they are now organized. For

[46] *Congressional Record*, March 10, 1969.

example, Stratton appealed to the AEC to withhold a construction permit on the basis of thermal effects; and, in doing so, he publicly called attention to the fact that the AEC was limited to considering only radiological effects. He then appealed to Governor Rockefeller to require installation of cooling towers to protect the lake. The response was: "The State water classification system is designed to safeguard our waters by assuring that the rights of all interested parties are adequately protected." Stratton called this "pretty thin stuff . . . you just can't look out for everybody concerned with equal fervor and get anywhere." [47]

Other evidence presented at the Stockmeister hearings supported Stratton's concern over conflicting interests. In an exchange of letters in the fall of 1968 between the Department of Health and representatives of the CSCL, the department stated its position as follows: "The State Health Department looks on Cayuga Lake as a valuable asset to the State and therefore is interested in protecting it. On the other side of the coin, the State Health Department is involved in the industrial development of the State." [48] And, later: "Since the company has begun construction it apparently seems that it can meet our requirements concerning its discharge." [49]

The case was brought up again, in January 1969, at

[47] *Rochester Democrat-Chronicle*, September 18, 1968.

[48] Letter from Dwight F. Metzler, Deputy Commissioner of the New York State Department of Health, to William Ward (August 28, 1968).

[49] Letter from Ronald S. Bratspis, New York State Department of Health, on request of Governor Rockefeller, to Mrs. John H. Lehman (October 17, 1968).

hearings of the Senate Standing Committee on Public Utilities and, in February and March, at hearings of the New York State Water Resources Commission (WRC) on proposed thermal criteria. The latter were hearings at which the Water Resources Commission presented its recommendations concerning the thermal criteria to be used as guidelines by the New York State Department of Health in its permit-issuing capacity. At these hearings, Associated Industries, a lobby which acts for utilities and manufacturing industries, urged weaker standards. This position was rebutted by a Cornell group which included both critics of Bell Station and scientists involved in the NYSE&G-supported study, all of whom were concerned about the inadequacy of the criteria. The standards proposed by the WRC were regarded as a defeat for conservationists. They permitted discharge that would raise surface temperatures up to 3° F. beyond a radius of three hundred feet, but would not restrict the pumping activities which some viewed as "an extreme and unjustified threat to deep-stratified lakes."[50] The possibility of investigating specific cases where these conditions were inadequate was left open; but once standards were established, the "burden of proof" concerning damage rested with the public. The New York State Department of Health accepted the proposed standards, but the Federal Water Pollution Control Administration has yet to approve them. Acceptance by the FWPCA remains questionable, for al-

[50] Letter by Franklin Moore to *Ithaca Journal* (March 18, 1969).

though there are no federal regulations as to the maximum area which can be heated, there are specific limitations to heating the hypolimnion.

Assemblywoman Cook and Senator Day were prompted by the above events to introduce in the state legislature three bills of direct relevance to the future of Cayuga Lake. The first gave the WRC greater powers to subclassify state waters, using different standards for lakes than for streams, and recommended lake standards for thermal and radioactive discharges. This bill passed the Assembly with one dissenting vote and the Senate unanimously, but was later vetoed by the Governor. The second bill would have prevented site excavation and other expenditures prior to the issuance of a permit. This was to avoid the kind of investment made by the NYSE&G, with its implications for pressuring the permit-granting agencies and its potential cost to the consumer. Although the bill passed both Senate and Assembly unanimously, it was also vetoed.

The third bill would have limited radioactive discharges to concentrations no greater than 50 per cent above company estimates as filed in the Preliminary Safety Analysis Report submitted by the NYSE&G to the AEC. This passed the Assembly unanimously, but was not allowed to get on the Senate calendar. The intense lobbying by Associated Industries of New York State on behalf of the utilities was a factor here. They criticized the limitations as arbitrary and threatening to the state's nuclear power development program. Governor Rockefeller may also have been negatively influenced by the possible jurisdictional conflicts with the AEC over radiological standards.

The Governor justified his use of the veto by declaring the bills "premature" in view of the fact that the state was, at the time, formulating an integrated package to safeguard the environment. On May 29, 1969, in his release concerning the veto, Rockefeller noted that among those recommending veto of the bills were the State Department of Health, the Water Resources Commission, the Department of Commerce, the Office for Local Government, the Office of Planning Coordination, the Power Authority, the Atomic and Space Development Authority, Associated Industries, and the Chamber of Commerce. Later, State Senator Thomas McGowan, chairman of the Standing Committee on Public Utilities, was to claim that the bills would not have passed through the state legislature in the first place, if there had been any expectation that they might be signed into law.[51] Thus, initial efforts at the state level to deal with situations such as the Bell Station case via legislation were unsuccessful. Nearly a year later, Governor Rockefeller did submit the reorganization plan which created a Department of Environmental Conservation to coordinate environmental programs. But state legislation remains at a more general level than that proposed by the three bills blocked in May 1969.

The political turmoil at the state level at the time these bills were pending created a great deal of uncer-

[51] *Nucleonics Week*, June 26, 1969.

tainty concerning the criteria on water-quality standards that the NYSE&G would have to meet. Furthermore, in early April 1969 it was clear that the company-sponsored scientific reports on Cayuga Lake would not be rapidly forthcoming with conclusive results. In view of this state of affairs, William A. Lyons, the NYSE&G president, decided to postpone activity on the construction permit application to the AEC. On April 11 he formally recommended an indefinite postponement to the Board of Directors "to provide more time for additional research on cooling systems for thermal discharge from the plant and for consideration of the economic effects of such systems." [52] He projected a possible two- or three-year delay, noting that an equivalent facility must be completed by no later than 1976.

This crucial decision has several interesting aspects. First, the AEC application was "postponed" but not "withdrawn." This means that it can be resurrected with minimum delay at any time, without the formalities of a reapplication. Second, although a communications committee of twelve managers from various departments and branches of the company had been discussing the issue at regular meetings, the decision appears to have been made by Lyons alone. It was not made on the basis of concern about AEC approval; for precedent indicated that the AEC may require modifications, but does not deny permits. Lyons, in essence,

[52] William A. Lyons, statement to the NYSE&G Board of Directors, April 11, 1969.

chose to halt the normal process of application, in response to political activity not directly related to the application process.

The losses involved in shifting the construction timetable were concrete and predictable. They involved diverting those involved in developing various phases of the operation to other activities. The company had to establish terms of contract with suppliers and contractors, and lost their place in line in ordering components with long lead times. Delay, on the other hand, had certain advantages in avoiding a number of possible problems. Such a move, it was hoped, would correct biased impressions promulgated by critics, avoid conflict, and clarify future costs which were, at the time, uncertain. By postponing rather than withdrawing application, it was hoped to minimize losses in design and engineering efforts.

The decision of the NYSE&G to delay spawned another citizens' group. Thirty-five members of the Lansing business community met in late April to form the Citizens Committee to Save Bell Station.[53] The informal group, whose spokesmen were the vice-president of a highway materials company, the First Ward Supervisor of Lansing, a grocery store owner, and an insurance man, met three times to discuss the issue. Their main activity was to post a petition in about seventy-five locations, including union halls, local business and town offices, reading: "We the undersigned of the area involved, having faith in the Electric and Gas Cor-

[53] *Ithaca Journal*, April 29, 1969.

poration, its employees, the Federal and State regulatory agencies governing licensing of nuclear-powered generating stations, pledge our support to the planned project of Bell Station." It was estimated by one of the organization's spokesmen that about 2,000 signatures were collected.

Another response came from the Tompkins County Board of Supervisors, the group of county representatives which had originally encouraged the NYSE&G to site Bell Station on Cayuga Lake. On June 24, 1969, the board voted to ask the NYSE&G to renew its planning on Bell Station. Edward P. Abbott, chairman for Planning and Public Relations of the board at this time, said at the meeting that "certain organized groups have sought to discredit the New York Electric and Gas Company with the result that a situation verging on panic exists, making calm and rational discussion almost impossible." [54] This response apparently represented a concern for the economic impact of the new station and a reaction against increased government regulation. Abbott was also chairman of the Cayuga Lake Basin Board, which, as a part of their planning activities, had contracted a firm of consulting engineers to do a $100,000 study on water needs of the area. The study advised that the area go to Cayuga Lake for water, but the CLBB was reluctant to accept this advice, and subsequently declared its plans to use two local creeks instead of the lake for an eventual water reservoir.[55] In this light, the planning

[54] *Ibid.*, June 24, 1969.
[55] *Ibid.*, February 25, 1970.

body may not have considered the purity of the lake water of prime importance in its water management projections.

Parenthetically, Abbott's comment with respect to the activity of citizens' groups represents a more general sentiment. Glenn Seaborg, AEC Chairman, referring to public criticism which "stacks the deck" against nuclear power plants, spoke of "the technique of taking all the detrimental, isolated facts and information about a subject, misinterpreting other factual materials, adding numerous statements—taken out of context—by authorities in the field, and placing all this material in a story that gives a completely one-sided viewpoint. . . . Such dishonesty is made more harmful by the fact that these articles are written as exposés and crusades in the public interest."[56]

The CSCL responded to the postponement of Bell Station by relaxing the pace of its activities, though the Executive Committee continued to build contacts and legal support for an eventual AEC hearing. Plans were formulated to reorganize into problem-oriented committees to consider general problems such as the nutrients fed to the lake by agriculture, pesticides, municipal sewage, and recreation.

[56] Quoted in USAEC, *Nuclear Power, Facts instead of Fiction* (Washington, June 1969), p. 12.

IV / *Salient Issues*

As the Cayuga Lake case developed, four interdependent levels of activity were evident. The NYSE&G plans evoked a response, both supportive and negative, from the scientific community. A citizens' group, developed from the response of scientists, and the articulate activities of the group influenced the further behavior of concerned scientists as well as the decisions of the company. A background level of political activity bears closely on the events in the controversy.

These four levels of activity are outlined in Table 7. The interrelationships between them will become more apparent in examining several dimensions of the case which merit analysis beyond the particular situation of Bell Station. These are the economic options of an expanding utility, the unresolved technical questions, the behavior of scientists in a public controversy, and the implications for public policy.

Economic Options of an Expanding Utility

Decisions of the company at each stage of the controversy were based on a combination of economic fac-

Table 7. Cayuga Lake Bell Station controversy, chronology of major events, 1968 and 1969

A. *Major events 1968*

	June 1967	January	February	March	April	June
NYSE&G	Original announcement of Cayuga Lake site.	Site purchased. Workshop with CLBB. Press announcement.	Distributed fact sheet. Participation in WRC seminar. Selected Company of the Year by Tompkins County Chamber of Commerce.	Applied for AEC construction permit.	Began site clearance. Awarded research contract to CAL.	Awarded research contract to Cornell WRC.
Scientific activity — NYSE&G-supported				Cornell WRC proposals for study of Cayuga Lake submitted to NYSE&G.		Cornell WRC receives research contract.
Independent			Cornell WRC seminar.	Eipper committee formed.	Engineering committee formed.	Eipper report.
Citizens' activity				First exchange of letters between concerned citizens and NYSE&G.		
Relevant hearings and legislative events					Hearings, U.S. Senate subcommittee on Air and Water Pollution, Committee on Public Works. Statements submitted by Ithaca citizens.	

	July	August	September	October	November	December
			Press release responding to Eipper report.			
		Carlson committee formed.		Krumhansl proposal. Scientists' letter to Dept. of Health proposing lake standards.		Carlson report.
	CLPA statement asking delay of construction.	Eipper calls meeting of concerned citizens.	CSCL formed and organized. Monthly open meetings begin.			CSCL meeting to discuss possibility of legal intervention.
			Joint Legislative Committee on Consumer Protection. Assemblywoman Cook argues NYSE&G site clearance unnecessary consumer expense.		Joint Legislative Committee on Conservation, Ithaca, N.Y. NYSE&G and CSCL participate.	

Table 7. (continued)

B. *Major events 1969*

	January	February	March	April	May
NYSE&G	Press release responding to Carlson report. Ad hoc committee formed to study controversy. First direct exchange with CSCL.	Sent radiological expert from California to to speak to CSCL. Meeting of business, government and labor representatives.		Postponement announced to Board of Directors.	
Scientific activity					
NYSE&G-supported				Cornell WRC research terminated. Funding from NYSE&G ceased.	
Independent		Engineering committee study released.			
Citizens' activity	NYSE&G presents position at CSCL meeting. Ballot on intervention approved. Green retained.			Citizens Committee to Save Bell Station formed.	
Relevant hearings and legislative events	Hearing by Senate Committee on Public Utilities.	Water Resources Commission hearings, Albany, Buffalo, Syracuse, White Plains, to establish recommendations on standards. CSCL participates.	Cook, Day bills pass state legislature.		Rockefeller vetoes Cook, Day bills.

June	July	August	September	October	November
Asked by Tompkins County Board of Supervisors to renew planning.					
			Cornell WRC report on ecology of lake.		CAL report on thermal properties of lake.
	CSCL builds contacts and legal support for eventual hearing.			Memo to FWPCA to object to health department standards.	
	Health Dept. accepts standards recommended by Water Resources Commission.				

tors and political considerations. The options available at various points of decision are shown in Figure 4.

The original decision to locate on Cayuga Lake was based on the need for corporate growth, on the availability of a cold water supply, and on the central location with respect to distribution to the New York State

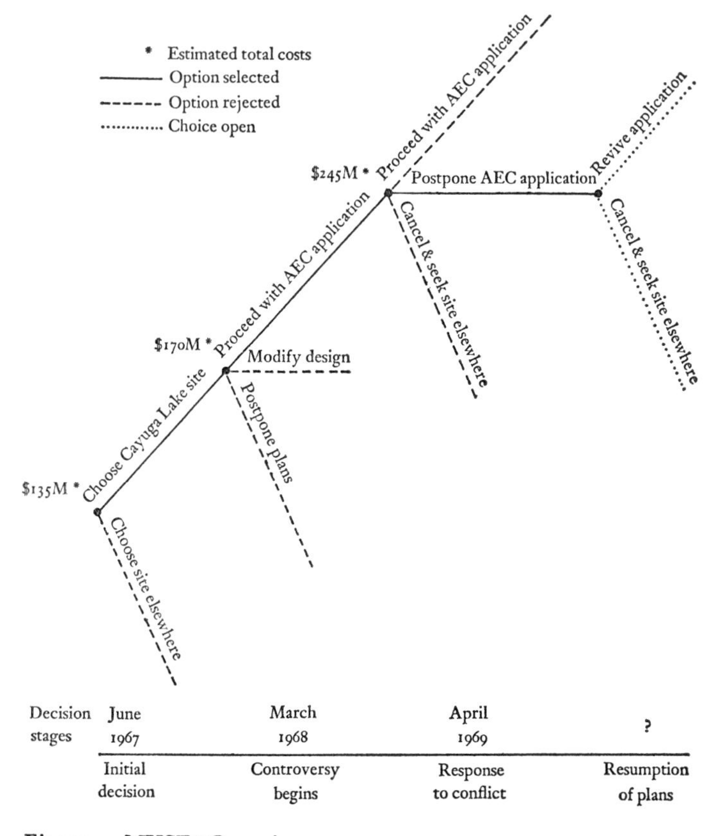

Figure 4. NYSE&G options

transmission grid. In economic terms, critics of Bell Station saw this decision as one in which benefits would accrue to the NYSE&G and to people through the state at a "cost" to the 30,000 people in the lake region, a view which was reinforced by the company's plans to sell about 70 per cent of its power to Consolidated Edison in New York City.[1] From the utility's perspective, it was necessary to expand plant capacity well in advance of future demands so that excess power, sold one year for use to outside territories, could be available for local distribution when the need arose.

The options available in March 1968 included accepting the design modifications recommended by critics to minimize damage to the lake. Modifications to limit radionuclide escape were estimated to add $500,000 in construction costs and $100,000 per year in operating costs; those proposed to limit thermal pollution—natural draft cooling towers—were estimated by the NYSE&G to cost $21.3 million initial investment, and to add $2.4 million to the annual operating cost of power production. This is less than 10 per cent of production costs, excluding administration, transmission, and other expenses not directly involved in production. The NYSE&G estimate of the cost of cooling towers was questioned on the basis of experience elsewhere. The Vermont Yankee Corporation claimed that cooling towers

[1] *Nucleonics Week*, January 16, 1969. Overlooked by many critics was the NYSE&G's stated intention to use its excess power capability within its own territory, as soon as local demand increased.

for its 540-MWe plant would cost $6.5 million, plus $900,000 in annual operating costs. Maine Yankee Corporation estimated a cost of from five to ten million dollars for cooling towers for its 830-MWe reactor. An economist, Jeff Romm, suggested several reasons for this disparity.[2] He saw no indication that the company sought to adapt the total design to the addition of cooling towers, a failure which would lead to unnecessary expense. Romm also claimed the NYSE&G evaluated the reduction of productive capacity with the use of cooling towers at too high a cost. Finally, it appeared to Romm that in reaching the estimate of $21.3 million, the company did not, as it claimed, calculate its costs on the basis of the actual expenses of cooling tower operation. Rather, he calculated that this high figure included the sale value of electricity lost due to capacity reduction.

Based on the NYSE&G estimate, the additional costs would be passed on to the consumer at an average rate increase of only $5.00 or $6.00 per year. Nevertheless, the company chose not to modify the design of the unit, the capital cost of which was, by this time, projected by the NYSE&G to have increased from $135 million to $170 million.

The next point of decision was reached in April 1969. The company management, reacting to political activity, officially postponed its plans, a move which they

[2] Jeff Romm, *The Cost of Cooling Towers for Bell Station* (Cornell University Water Resources and Marine Sciences Center, March 1969 (mimeographed).

expected would raise the estimated total cost of the plant to about $245 million. At some future point, the NYSE&G will have to decide whether to proceed with its application for a construction permit or to site elsewhere.

An interesting question is raised by these decisions. Why was the company reluctant to adopt the recommended design changes and pass this cost on to the consumer? A number of factors enter into their rejection of this option. First, the company asserted that the information about cooling towers and their environmental effects in similar climatic conditions was inadequate; fogging and icing were likely possibilities.[3] Second, they pointed out the aesthetic problem of large towers on the shoreline of the lake. They claimed that their reluctance was based not so much on costs as on reports which suggested that natural draft towers posed problems as serious as did the once-through cooling system they replaced. Uncertainty about environmental effects of other cooling systems precluded their consideration.

A number of social and economic considerations entered into the reluctance to modify the plant design, such as pressure within the industry to resist public demands, and the lingering threat of pressure from the state-owned utility. Utilities hesitate to raise rates. Doing so requires negotiation with the Public Service Commission, a process initiated by the NYSE&G in April 1970 for the first time in ten years, when it applied for

[3] William A. Lyons, statement to the NYSE&G Board of Directors, April 11, 1969.

a rate increase of 10–12 per cent in order to meet the rising costs of financing new facilities.[4] Regulated by the Public Service Commission, utilities have had little choice but to design for minimum cost and to be concerned with construction costs as narrowly defined by minimum required standards. Long conditioned to this state of affairs, and fearing closer regulation, they see it in their best interests to keep rates as low as possible. Reasonable rates are sacred; the utilities' public image (and continued existence as a regulated monopoly) rest on a philosophy of adequate service at as low a cost as possible.

Finally, a question of trust appears to have been involved in the reluctance to modify the plant design. Company management was disillusioned and upset by the controversy, and sought to avoid further involvement. Conflict hardened their position. They responded by adopting an inflexible position which was to prove costly. It was anticipated by the company that even if they agreed to modifications, they would be attacked by the CSCL on some other ground. That the CSCL publicly predicated its entire strategy on opposition only to the particular design of Bell Station, not to nuclear plants in general, did not assuage the company's anxiety; although compliance with CSCL demands would certainly have called into question the credibility of any subsequent attack.

Though the NYSE&G management argued throughout the controversy that criticism was premature and

[4] *Ithaca Journal*, April 15, 1970.

that their plans were subject to change, design modifications would require the additional time and complexity of filing an amendment to their five-volume *Preliminary Safety Analysis Report* and their AEC application. Thus there was incentive to limit the number of changes.

These factors were sufficiently compelling for the NYSE&G management to reject, in April 1969, the alternative of modifying the design of the plant. Remaining future alternatives were either to build as originally planned—if a permit could be acquired—or to build units with equivalent capacity in another less controversial site. The rejection of cooling towers, it must be noted, was not necessarily a final decision. In February 1970 the management claimed to interpret the research reports as being favorable to their original plans.[5] But, at a meeting in April, a company information specialist claimed that if investigations proved the plant would harm the lake, cooling towers would have to be installed.[6] Whatever their decision, management anticipates that costs of electricity will increase along with pressure to consider environmental problems.

The course of events in this case suggests that the NYSE&G and perhaps the industry in general have been slow to respond to the political pressures which are now forcing them to consider alternatives. One source of resistance is connected with the character of hierarchical organizations in which decisions are made centrally by

[5] *Nuclear Industry*, 17, 2, February 1970.
[6] *Ithaca Journal*, April 22, 1970.

a few people. Utilities have been highly successful in dealing with their narrowly defined and predictable set of problems; electricity is perhaps the only commodity which has actually not increased in price over the past ten years. Sustained success, with minimum challenge, however, tends to petrify structure. This is reflected in the difficulty experienced by power companies in recruiting engineers from good modern engineering schools; for the work has tended to be conservative and routine. Hierarchical organizations characteristically find it difficult to respond to outside pressures and have limited adaptive capacity to meet the kinds of broad problems posed by the political and technical uncertainties involved in the present case.[7] Consultants working with NYSE&G engineers, for example, felt they were "manipulated from above." "We would ask a question and the answer would come back two days later after someone else approved it." With respect to the State Health Department water-quality standards (see p. 48) NYSE&G engineers were unable to respond immediately to the compromise proposal. Although they were later to agree with it, their delayed response served to intensify the polarization which was developing.

[7] There is a great deal of literature in the field of organizational theory concerned with the types of organizational structures which are sufficiently flexible to accommodate themselves to rapid change, obsolescence of knowledge, and uncertainty. See, for example, Victor Thompson, *Modern Organization* (New York: Alfred Knopf, 1963) and Warren Bennis and P. E. Slater, *The Temporary Society* (New York: Harper and Row, 1968).

The options selected by the company in response to the controversy were rational, from the point of view of the company's own narrow objectives. There was no economic rationale for the NYSE&G to internalize any of the costs involved with protecting a public resource. As long as there is no public policy concerning responsibility for externalities, there is no incentive for a company to assume this responsibility. Yet, the difficulties of the NYSE&G in responding to its critics and in dealing with uncertain technical dimensions, contributed to the controversy. These difficulties reflect a political ineptitude stemming, in part, from the character of the company's organizational structure. The NYSE&G's top-level positions, as of January 1969, are (1) President, (2) Comptroller, (3) Secretary and Treasurer, (4) Senior Vice President of Rates and Regulations, (5) Vice President of Administration, (6) Vice President of Purchasing, (7) Vice President of Operation and Production, (8) Vice President and Chief Engineer, and (9) Manager of Public Relations. These positions were occupied by persons close to retirement age, who had been with the company a long time. The fact that there are no formal long-range planning or market research positions suggests that change and flexibility are not given special consideration by the company.

Another source of inflexibility is the narrow perspective of utilities—a perspective which does not consider the possibility that fulfilling one public need may create yet another. From this point of view, the conscientious and successful provision of services in itself justifies the means of providing such services. This orientation leads inevitably to minimizing consideration of externalities such as the social and environmental issues which generated this controversy. Company management sincerely believes their activities warrant acceptance by their customers; and, as evidence, they point to their research, their service, and their efforts to construct architecturally aesthetic buildings and underground facilities. Only recently has the industry felt it necessary to give attention to public information, claiming that not more than 10–15 per cent of electrical customers would disapprove of nuclear power projects.[8] Indeed, the NYSE&G perceived the present controversy in highly particular terms, as the result of agitation by a few "militants" and not as a serious challenge with long-range implications.

Despite their concern with maintaining a good public image, their speeches, delayed responses to criticism, and actual decisions suggest that, a victim of its organizational style, the industry is incapable of responding readily to the kinds of pressure confronting it with respect to environmental issues.

Unresolved Technical Questions

Ecological systems defy rapid, systematic, and definitive analysis; conclusive answers to technical questions are often impossible. Uncertainty concerning such questions underlies the Bell Station controversy and has cru-

[8] Electric Utility Industry Task Force, *op. cit.*, p. 26. In this case, the "anti-business bias" of Cornell University was considered partly responsible for generating the controversy.

cial bearing on the decisions relating to the siting of power plants. Despite this uncertainty, the growing number of controversies similar to the Cayuga Lake case indicates that public policy concerning the development of electrical power will have to deal systematically with environmental problems.

A striking aspect of the studies relating to this case was the difficulty in acquiring data from which to draw definitive, quantitative conclusions.

> The reader is again reminded of certain cautionary notes sounded throughout this report. The importance of considering extremes as well as averages, the naturally great temporal and spatial variability of biological systems, the size of the lake being studied, the short duration of the present investigation, and the incompleteness and/or unreliability of those investigations conducted previously, are all factors adding to the difficulty of drawing readily quantifiable conclusions.[9]

The technical problems, then, could not be conclusively resolved, owing to lack of knowledge of the ecology of lake systems and consequent uncertainty about the effect of the power plant. This uncertainty was partly due to the inadequacy of data available on relevant parameters of the problem. There was little basis on which significant normal trends over time could be evaluated.[10] Some of the areas of uncertainty can be briefly indicated.

[9] Oglesby, *op. cit.*, p. 450.

[10] Ironically, about fifteen years ago a graduate student proposed writing his thesis on the effects of Milliken Station at the time of its construction, but was discouraged from doing so by his adviser.

There is, for example, no adequate theory for the establishment or maintenance of the thermocline, which is fundamental to understanding the lake's stratification pattern and the system of nutrient and heat exchange. The nature of the stresses at the interface between the heated plume and the underlying body of water are poorly understood. The effects of the pumping unit on the turbulence structure of the lake is unknown. Some suspect it could cause disturbance of rooted aquatic plants, or create internal waves affecting stratification. Finally—and this is a major argument presented by those claiming the discharge effect would be insignificant—it is difficult to isolate single effects on the nutrient content of the lake in view of the total residential and agricultural situation in the lake drainage area. It was pointed out that there are about 132 locations around Cayuga Lake that are classified as polluted for human bathing. Many lakes-shore cottages dump wastes directly into the lake, and an estimated 2,500 people in the drainage basin live in nonsewered municipal areas. The agricultural and dairy industries bordering the lake release about 725,000 tons of animal waste and 33,000 tons of fertilizer to the soil annually.

The argument concerning the difficulty in isolating the sources of eutrophication crystallized around a projected cattle-feeding station on the west shore of Cayuga Lake. It was originally planned to drain the wastes from this station into the lake. The possible effect of increasing the number of cattle from 2,000 to 10,000 was estimated to be equivalent to increasing the population of a town from 20,000 to 100,000. In comparison, it was argued, the effect of the power plant would be negligible.

The importance of the above arguments rests on the issue of the eutrophication of the lake. The eutrophication process is one in which the capacity of a lake to produce organic growth is increasing. The effect of Bell Station is of concern because of the heavy supply of nutrients drained into the lake from the surrounding agricultural and residential areas. Critics feared that the pumping and heating effects of the plant would serve to create conditions in which these nutrients would foster algal growth instead of settling in the bottom sediment. They argued that if Bell Station were to contribute to the eutrophication process of Cayuga Lake, this process would be virtually irreversible.

The question of irreversibility is fundamental to the controversy and one difficult to resolve. A member of the FWPCA noted four ways to prevent eutrophication, the first being the most important: (1) limiting fertility, (2) utilizing food chains to improve lakes, (3) stimulating parasites to kill off aquatic plants, and (4) using toxic chemicals to kill algae.[11] Tests recently conducted at Cornell on experimental ponds suggest that if fertilization of a lake were to cease, eutrophication could be reversed.[12] And, in an actual case, the diversion

[11] A. F. Bartsch, qouted in *Environmental Science and Technology*, April, 1970, p. 270.

[12] Directed by Hugh F. Mulligan at Cornell University (personal communication).

of sewage away from Lake Washington in Seattle effectively reduced algal growth. The Cornell pond studies suggest that there is a linear relationship between the amount of nutrients added to a body of water and the extent of algal growth. Thus, to reverse the process of eutrophication of Cayuga Lake would involve systematic reduction of the nutrient content. There are difficulties, however. The character of development on the Lake Washington shore permitted a comparatively complete system of diverting, by trunk line, sewage and other wastes to Puget Sound. Moreover, the lake is located at the foot of a mountainous area, so that there were flushing effects which helped to clear it. Bell Station critics claim that costs of reversing eutrophication in the case of Cayuga Lake would be prohibitive, for it would be virtually impossible to remove the nutrient sources.

There was little public discussion, by critics, of the Cornell eutrophication experiments going on at the time and of their implications for Cayuga Lake, although Hugh F. Mulligan, the principal investigator in these experiments, had signed the Eipper report. Nor was there serious consideration, by critics, of the possible relevance of the proposal made by Krumhansl and others to use the power plant to reverse eutrophication.

Technical uncertainty was also a problem with respect to the issue of radiological hazards. For example, when James Smith, the NYSE&G consultant from General Electric, referred to company specifications at the November 1968 hearings, he claimed that the expected radio-isotopes in the discharge were well within AEC permissible limitations, and would have concentrations "truly insignificant." [13] A critic at the hearings countered that he preferred to deal with legal restrictions than with company "promises." He then questioned the meaning of "safety" and "risk," claiming that AEC permissible concentrations were based on available but inadequate knowledge which was currently under some question.[14] LaMont Cole, a Cornell ecologist, has argued "there are great areas of unknowns. . . . We don't know just what paths radionuclides will take in food chains. . . . The evidence is that there is no threshhold for radiation effects so you have to choose arbitrary standards." [15] Cole's conclusion is that because there is no way to measure damage, the optimal amount of radiation discharge should be zero.

The short-term studies stimulated directly by the controversy added little to resolve uncertainty, and technical issues were not clarified by critics who interpreted data to justify their original fears. The data which researchers interpreted to indicate that the effects of the power station would be insignificant relative to other

[13] Hearings, November 22, 1968, *op. cit.*, morning question and answer period.

[14] For example, John W. Gofman and Arthur R. Tamplin, two scientists from the Lawrence Radiation Laboratory, have suggested that radiation standards are too lax ("Environmental effects of producing electric power," *Hearings before the Joint Committee on Atomic Energy*, Part I, 91st Congress, 1969, pp. 604–746). This has become an issue in Minnesota, where the state is demanding the right to establish its own criteria.

[15] *Nucleonics Week*, April 3, 1969.

influences on the lake[16] were of little interest to critics; it was the possibility of irreversible damage which gave strength to their arguments, not the extent of damage

The patterns of controversy with respect to the radiological and the eutrophication issues were similar. In each case, one group asserted that the effect of Bell Station would be negligible, and the other tended to focus selectively on data supportive of their most dire anticipations, submerging a broader perspective which might have suggested alternatives Thus the controversy did not appear to be headed toward a resolution of the technical uncertainty.

The Behavior of the Scientific Community in a Public Controversy

As interest in the controversy grew and several scientists openly opposed the construction of Bell Station, the strains referred to earlier (p. 43) began to develop within the scientific community. This section will examine the source of these strains through analyzing the behavior of that community. At the outset, it is important to recognize that the disagreement among scientists was complex and subtle; it did not take the form of a rigid cleavage about substantive issues. We have seen, for example, that there was unanimity concerning the inadequacy of thermal standards established by the state. It was not a question of nuclear critics versus company stooges; nor was it a question of experts disagreeing on

[16] At worst, it was estimated, the damage to the lake would be equivalent to adding 1,000 people to the population of Ithaca.

the accuracy of each other's evidence. With one exception, that of a limnologist from another university who had for years been consulting for utilities, no scientist's professional expertise was called into question. And there is no evidence that the NYSE&G contracted for research with anything but responsible intentions. At the November hearings, Eipper referred to those working under NYSE&G contract and said:

> The credentials of these scientists are impeccable. I have complete confidence in these men, many of whom I have worked with for the past twenty years. There are some questions that the data are going to give rise to, and this is where the real credentials of the scientists come into play, not in the gathering of the data so much as in the interpretation of the data. . . . Who is going to *interpret* the data? [17]

On the one hand, critics clearly did not trust the NYSE&G to interpret objectively data for which it had contracted. On the other hand, many scientists involved in the case were concerned about the role of the scientist in the interpretation of inconclusive scientific data for use outside the profession.

There are several factors which help to explain this emphasis on interpretation. These relate to the character of scientific work and its bearing on the organization of the scientific community. First, for one scientist to take

[17] Stockmeister hearings, November 22, 1968, *op. cit.*, afternoon question and answer period.

issue with the validity of another's evidence would involve the task, impossible in this case, of duplicating the process of data-gathering. Second, sensitivity tends to intensify where the ethics concerning the appropriate role for scientists are ambiguous—that is, at the level of interaction in the political and economic arena. Although scientists and engineers often work on client-oriented problems, they prefer to resolve their technical arguments within the professional community. As soon as questionable data were interpreted in terms of their "significance" for practical problems, biases were suspected. It is understood among scientists that if science is conducted according to rules established outside the profession, it can no longer be considered objective or free from bias. Scientists are to test hypotheses objectively, provide facts, and avoid judgments or controversy. The testimony of one of the scientists working under NYSE&G contract expressed this point:

> I am one of the silent people who has been associated with data collection. . . . I am silent because I am busy collecting data. Members of the public, members of legislative bodies, will have to make the judgments. . . . We're not going to try to prove any points, we are testing hypotheses, and trying to be objective as we can, which is the reason why the group engaged in this study has avoided most of the public controversy.[18]

Of the several scientific groups involved in the controversy, the most active were the Water Resources

[18] *Ibid.*

Center study group doing scientific research under NYSE&G contract, and the Eipper and Carlson committees whose position papers and political activity were in opposition to the NYSE&G plans. The scope of inquiry of these groups was largely limited rather narrowly to the possible effects of the power plant on the lake. There was a conspicuous absence of a research

	Effect of plant on lake	Total lake environment
Position papers	Eipper Carlson	Krumhansl Cady Belcher-Linke
Research	NYSE&G-sponsored research Moore	X

Chart 2. Scope of inquiry in the Cayuga Lake case

strategy which would consider the total lake environment. The scope of inquiry encouraged in position papers and developed in research is summarized in Chart 2.

It is useful to explore the limitations of inquiry in the context of the activities of scientists who contributed in various ways to the case. These scientists engaged in four types of activity: research, development of a broad research strategy, policy analysis, and political action.

With the exception of research for the Moore report, most substantive research was performed under NYSE&G contract. This source of funding left researchers exposed to a great deal of criticism. Scientists in the NYSE&G-supported group claimed, however, that their source of funding would not affect their objectivity or detachment. Even the presence of utility engineers at meetings, described as "irritating at times," was denied to have influenced their work.[19] For applied scientists and engineers, industry-supported projects are often the core of research. They consider themselves able to cope with client demands and at the same time maintain the scientific validity of their work by persuading clients that the judgment of the scientific community is important. Like all scientists, they ultimately depend on professional peers for evaluation.[20] Outside influence such as public pressure or industrial objectives is strongly rejected. "What I am concerned about and very much concerned about, is any pressure on us at Cornell—the group that is doing this work—that we have a responsibility to provide *you* with the kinds of specific answers that you want." [21] Precautions were taken in the organization of the NYSE&G-sponsored report to protect

[19] It was claimed by one scientist that the company found it difficult to comprehend the necessity for uninfluenced research, and had the attitude that if a scientist is paid by a company his data should support company goals.

[20] Warren O. Hagstrom, *The Scientific Community* (New York: Basic Books, 1965), pp. 110 ff.

[21] Stockmeister hearings, November 22, 1968, *op. cit.*, afternoon question and answer period, statement by Professor Dworsky.

against bias. For example, to clarify responsibility, the reports were not combined, and each author signed his name to his own work. Yet, certain constraints were unavoidable. For example, the Cornell research group was not allowed to communicate directly with the CAL group, except through the company's design engineers. This limitation was imposed by the utility in a memo, ostensibly as a means of keeping the company engineers informed. Some participants felt that it was a means of control, however, and it posed difficulties in the scheduling and organization of research crucial to the collection of data.

Little energy was devoted to the second category of activity, the development of a broad research strategy. To some extent, the unexplored dimensions of the lake problem required discussion of an overall research agenda. This was evident in Cady's urging a study of the thermal effects on the lake as a whole, rather than on the limited area near the thermal discharge (see p. 48). It was also evident in Krumhansl's proposal to look at possible beneficiating effects of a power plant (see p. 50), in the Belcher-Linke alternatives, and in Oglesby's recommendations for further research. However, serious attention directed to developing a broad and coordinated research strategy tended to be restricted by the immediacy of the political issue, by the tentative character of the funding, and by the intermittent character of the research—a function of its dependence on short-term contracts awarded in response to the particular need. Because the research projects were short term, serious innovation in research design and organization was precluded. Although the problem called for an interdisciplinary strategy, time limitations and organizational constraints forced the work into a traditional disciplinary mold. In addition, serious attention to a broad research strategy was diverted by political activity, which kept the focus of attention on a narrow range of problems.

The third type of activity engaging the scientific community—policy analysis—was highly important in initially calling attention to the potential threat to the lake, and in stimulating both scientific research and political activity. The position papers of Eipper and Carlson were concerned primarily with raising issues which would otherwise have lain neglected; in this they were most successful. In their eagerness to raise necessary questions, however, they tended, in their reports, to overreach existing data and failed to differentiate between what was known to be a danger and what was merely questionable. The authors were criticized for their "nonscientific approach." It was suggested that their political focus led them to selective perception of data to the point of ignoring results of ongoing research which might contradict their position or allay public concern. Diaries containing raw data from the NYSE&G-sponsored research were made available to the critics, but according to the researchers their findings were not examined or discussed. Public statements of the critics, intended to inform, neglected to include material from current research on the possible reversibility of eutrophication. The technical alternatives proposed by Krumhansl, Linke, and Belcher were not seriously considered in the information disseminated by the critics who were concerned with political expediency. One of the dangers of such a selective focus, that it may limit the scope of inquiry, is especially important in the case of environmental issues, where popular sentiment tends to foster quick generalization and discourage the time-consuming process of weighing many alternatives.

The fourth type of activity engaged in by scientists was political. The issue of the lake was kept before the public through position papers, numerous speeches at schools, clubs, and meetings, and participation in citizens' committee activities. The effectiveness of these activities is evident in the success of the CSCL. At the same time, however, a number of people concerned with the future of Cayuga Lake considered that the approach of the critics was single-minded, led to public misinformation, and unnecessarily contributed to polarization over the issue. They regarded such an approach as obstructing consideration of constructive measures to "save the lake."

The nature and extent of the activities in which scientists chose to become involved depended basically on the scientists' perspective on the ethics of participating in controversial public issues. Some were criticized for taking an overt public position; others were criticized for thinking that it was possible to take a neutral position. The criticisms and justifications made of the activities of the two most vocal groups involved in the controversy turn on ethical points, as is evident from Table 8.

The concern with ethical problems of bias and interpretation, apparent in the table, is particularly operative in ecological sciences. While thrust into the thick of the environmental crisis, at this stage in their development they lack a tight theoretical structure to provide rigorous criteria for evaluation of scientific activity. This suggests that the divergence within the scientific community in this case was not based on disagreement concerning the importance of preserving the lake. Rather, it was rooted in differing perceptions as to what, in fact, are the "rules of the scientific game" within a controversial framework where the public interest is at stake. One group of scientists approached the problem as it would any other scientific problem, with objectivity and detachment as the basis of their "scientific credibility." Others perceived the problem as a moral issue, which therefore required their taking a philosophical and political position. They felt that their scientific credibility required assuming a public role.

Public activity leads a scientist into consideration of normative principles and moral issues. The concern is with what *ought* to be done, whereas science itself "can only chart the consequences of what *might* be done." [22] The tension between these norms, reflected in the

[22] John M. Ziman, *Public Knowledge* (Cambridge: At the University Press, 1968), p. 15.

Table 8. Criticism and justification in the Cayuga Lake case *

Groups criticized	Criticism	Justification
Opponents of Bell Station (Eipper report)	Taking a position destroys scientific credibility and is inappropriate. Reports were emotional and overstated. Subjective speculations based on selected data were presented as fact. They reflect personal interests in the lake. Taking a position on a public issue is all right, if it is clearly distinct from one's research.	Taking a position is necessary to provoke discussion and is necessary for "credibility." If scientists don't interpret their own data and thereby take a position, others will, with their own interests in mind. This is a philosophical issue where emotionalism is appropriate. Report, a position paper, was intended to raise issues, not to provide definitive answers. It was based on informed opinion. Accurate data on amount of eutrophication is not available, but is not relevant when effects irreversible.
Water Resources Center study group under NYSE&G contract (Oglesby-Allee report)	Report was bought by the company and was, therefore, necessarily biased and partisan. Outcome of report can determine future funding; for if the evidence discourages the siting of the project on the lake, there will be no further funding.† This makes a bias inevitable, especially considering present scarcity of research funds. The sampling was an inadequate basis for ultimate decisions made by the company, since its timing excluded part of the growing season.	All precautions were taken to ensure objectivity, e.g., report not shown to company until after publication, and each individual signed his own articles. In any case, review by scientific peers controls the honesty of scientists, who therefore cannot be bought. Research was a continuation of ongoing work: source of payment is irrelevant. Analysis was cut short for reasons of time and personnel, but solid technical data were carefully collected, and are therefore valid for future analysis.

* The list of criticisms and justifications was compiled from the comments of many different persons. Therefore, they are not always consistent. They do not necessarily suggest what one group of scientists has commented about the other.

† Employed on the project and paid out of NYSE&G funds were: eight laboratory assistants and technicians, five research assistants, one laborer, three typists, one programmer, six student assistants, two full-time research associates, and summer salaries for two professors.

scientific community, clearly poses a dilemma for scientists as they are drawn into the arena of public decision-making.

Policy Implications

The Cayuga Lake case points to a "policy gap" with respect to environmental issues. There are few broad principles or objectives on which to base a comprehensive program for balancing industrial development with other uses of the lake. Furthermore, existing mechanisms for implementing policy with respect to the regulation of utility development are better equipped to cope with traditional problems than to meet contingencies. There is a built-in tendency to maintain a functioning system, rather than to question it on the grounds of possible future problems such as those of concern to environmental critics. The case suggests that once standards are established, agencies tend to regard them as successful; there is a commitment to past decisions and a reluctance to make more than incremental changes

Let us examine the problems of the existing regulatory system and then consider the confusion in the objectives which underlie policy with respect to power generation and the environment. First, the administration of the existing regulatory system is highly fragmented. Each agency has a narrow and exclusive range of interests, a situation which makes multidimensional problems difficult to deal with. There is no regional agency with the power to coordinate and implement activity in the Lake Basin area and which can consider new development, such as a power plant, in the context of the complexity of agricultural, industrial and residential activity. Nor is there a multipurpose agency, concerned with the several problems posed by power plants. Jurisdiction is divided between the AEC and the State Health Department. Other agencies, with functionally related interests (such as the Department of Conservation), have little substantive authority to control matters of concern to them. Economic decisions which affect the amount the utility spends on its facilities are controlled by yet another agency, the Public Service Commission, recently criticized for creating the "most profitable utility industry in the nation at the expense of the consuming public." [23] An interesting manifestation of the tenuous character of the regulatory structure was the fact that the primary political activity in the Cayuga Lake case centered on the Stockmeister hearings. These hearings, which spotlighted the crucial issues and rallied political activity, were outside the normal application process. More serious than this fragmentation of jurisdiction is the conflict in the goals of each agency, reflecting the larger conflict between demands for increased power and the need for environmental protection. In this case, the eagerness to develop the nuclear power industry could have prevented a balanced decision, if the environmental interests had not been so effectively expressed. The letters from the health department (see p. 71),

[23] *New York Times*, March 5, 1969. The PSC has recently been reorganized to give greater attention to consumer and environmental issues.

for example, suggest the implications of conflicting concern with both industrial development and protection of the environment.[24] The AEC, too, has a dual function, both to promote nuclear development and to regulate it through the granting of licenses. This dual role was originally conceived as the basis of a vigorous civilian power program. Federal money in the amount of $2.3 billion was invested in research to develop commercially feasible atomic power. But the ability of the AEC to deal objectively with its conflicting functions of development and regulation is being seriously questioned in a growing number of controversies about the adequacy of AEC standards. New rulings proposed by the AEC in response to attacks on existing standards advised utilities to keep radiation releases as "low as practicable," a vague change which raises obvious questions of interpretation.

Recently, a new dimension has been added to the criticism. Senator George D. Aiken (Vermont Republican), a member of the Joint Committee on Atomic Energy, has raised the issue of AEC licensing practices, and has criticized the commission for fostering the tendency for "giant corporate utilities" to "monopolize and completely control" the development of nuclear power. Aiken has claimed that by continuing to license each plant as a research and development project—despite

[24] The dual concerns expressed by the health department are derived from its interpretation of Article 42, Section 1200 of the Public Health Law, which authorizes it to regulate for "reasonable" standards "consistent with public health and public enjoyment thereof, the propagation and protection of fish and wildlife . . . and the industrial development of the State."

their obvious commercial value—the AEC protects utilities from antitrust regulation. Once utilities have a research operation license, they then "go down the street to the Security and Exchange Commission and obtain permission to sell stock on the basis of the profits they anticipate."[25] Aiken's criticism highlights the overriding concern of the AEC with development.

Controversy and criticism have caused evident frustration within the AEC. AEC Commissioner James Ramey claims that "in our judgment these criticisms are not justified, and many are irresponsible. . . . We believe that existing standards provide a high degree of protection to the public"[26] A more extreme expression of frustration is in a publicized letter written by ex-AEC Commissioner Frank Costagliola to the president of Cornell and to other universities. Costagliola expressed his concern with the "small academic groups who are tending to degrade the competence of the AEC in the eyes of the public. . . . It is my opinion that the access our colleges and universities have to federal funds for the conduct of research is a privilege not a right."[27]

Policy concerning the regulation of utility development is formulated on the basis of a set of principles and objectives supported by scientific and economic data. We have seen that scientific information very often lends itself to varying interpretations. Warner Schilling

[25] Senator George D. Aiken, quoted in *New York Times*, March 5, 1970.

[26] *Ithaca Journal*, March 28, 1970.

[27] *Nucleonics Week*, June 29, 1969.

suggests that one of the problems posed by the entry of scientists into the public policy process is that those who make policy decisions must often choose a course of action in the face of conflicting interpretation by scientists.[28] Indeed, one source of the difficulties of regulation is that decisions must be made where casual links between the effects of plant design and changes in the environment cannot be definitively established. The inconclusiveness of scientific evidence is such that the granting of permits is rather like an insurance game, examining probabilities and focusing on risk and protection rather than on seeking "right answers."

As for economic data, information concerning the value of a resource may contribute to policy decisions, but there remains uncertainty in this area as well. An attempt was made to estimate the value of the lake by looking at its various uses as a recreation facility, a municipal and industrial water supply, a basin for municipal waste disposal, and a general environmental resource. Values attached to these uses were based, for example, on rental values of property, on the costs of an outing using the lake, and on the "transfer costs," defined as the cost of doing the activity elsewhere. An annual value of between $6 million and $10.9 million was arrived at in terms of present use.[29] This extraordinarily

[28] Warner R. Schilling, "Scientists, Foreign Policy, and Politics," in Robert Gilpin and Christopher Wright (eds.), *Scientists and National Policy Making* (New York: Columbia University Press, 1964), pp. 148–149.

[29] David Allee, "Uses and Values of Cayuga Lake," in Oglesby, *op. cit.*, pp. 424–434.

low figure sharply reveals the inadequacy of traditional economic analysis to deal with the total value of a natural resource. For the marginal value of a lake, estimated on the basis of use, is considerably less than the minimum which would be required to compensate individuals if they were deprived of its use. Estimates of total value must take into account the uniqueness of a resource, as well as changing tastes and preferences which may determine future uses.

These are questions which have social impact; and here, as in the case of scientific criteria, one is dealing with uncertain variables. For example, if there is a change in the quality of lake water, what effect would this have on recreational demand? How does one distribute or trade off various uses of the lake equitably? Assuming that power stations must be built somewhere, how does one distribute pollution costs? It has been argued in this case that Cayuga Lake is less polluted than other lakes, and that Bell Station is therefore no cause for concern. Does this imply there should be an equity in pollution distribution? Finally, and perhaps most difficult to quantify, there is the value attached to keeping options open for future uses of the lake. What is it worth today to have available the option to use the lake in the future in unknown ways? One may project future population and income growth, and calculate possible future uses of the lake; but the option value of the lake—particularly if damage through thermal pollution is irreversible—is a crucial and nonmeasurable variable. One economist has stated the problem as being akin to the dynamic programming problem which requires a present action (which may violate conventional benefit-cost criteria) to be compatible with the attainment of future states of affairs. But we know little about the value that the instrumental variables may take . . . and about the quantitative significance of the asymmetry in the implications of technological advances . . . for producing industrial goods on the one hand and natural environments on the other.[30]

Beyond the economic and scientific data, the question still remains as to what, in fact, are the basic public policy objectives in a case of this nature. Two principles have been emphasized by environmentalists, and both have potential dangers. The first is that the "burden of proof" should be placed on utilities to guarantee effective protection against possible damage. Damage to the environment, it is argued, is an externality, the cost of which is borne not by a utility, but by the public. On the other hand, utilities operate on the basis that there is no economic justification for assuming the additional expense of maximum environmental protection, until the necessity for such protection is definitively established. Externalities are clearly involved in this case; however, the "burden of proof" argument loses much of its validity if one considers that if the NYSE&G were to assume responsibility for pollution control, it could pass economic costs on to the customers through rate increases. Thus, the public ultimately would bear the cost. Fur-

[30] John V. Krutilla, "Conservation Reconsidered," *American Economic Review*, 57, 4, September 1967, p. 785.

thermore, since the present rate structure favors larger users, this cost would constitute a tax which would be borne disproportionately by lower income groups.

The second principle, and a much more fundamental one, is that unrestricted economic growth is no longer a viable objective. Environmentalists question whether the present rapid growth of the power industry is inevitable or indeed desirable. Is there a saturation point in economic growth and increased consumer demand? In the past, it has been assumed that maximum possible growth is optimal, and industry has had little or no constraint on directing its own growth. In line with this assumption, NYSE&G practices are very much oriented to fostering the 7 per cent annual increase in electricity demand that they regard as inevitable. Rates decline with increased use of electricity, rewarding the large consumer. Brochures are circulated, encouraging conversion to electric heat and air-conditioning. Occasional promotional activities include giving away electric blankets with each purchase of an electric dryer. The extent to which promotional activity bears on the increase in electricity demand is questionable, since it is both a symptom and a cause of the assumption of continued maximum economic growth. It is this assumption which is brought into question by the Cayuga Lake case. Here, again, the short-range solutions to this problem suggested by environmentalists may create yet further dilemmas. For retarding economic growth may well have a regressive social effect, blocking economic mobility and leading to further social unrest. One concludes that policy with respect to environmental issues may have broad-ranging political, economic, and social implications, and must be developed with appreciation for the fact that "an ecological perspective" is at least as important in the political sphere as in the scientific.

Conclusion

The Cayuga Lake case illustrates the recent contention of environmental analysts that it is imperative not to consider technological application myopically, neglecting its secondary consequences.[1] The complex set of technical, economic and political questions raised by the case implies the need for coordinated regulatory activities on the local, state, and federal levels. Coordination requires clear policy concerning the extent to which economic growth and increased use of electric power should continue to be encouraged. This policy should generate a set of guidelines concerning the regulation of utility expansion and the responsibility for environmental protection. And policy must be made with a view to broader social concerns, so that the inevitable costs of environmental protection are equitably distributed.

The case further suggests the need for early assessment of the development of technology. If thermal pollution had been thought to be a limiting factor at the

[1] See, for example, Harold Gilliam, "The Fallacy of Single Purpose Planning," *Daedalus 96*, 4, Fall 1967, pp. 1142–1157.

time of the commercial development of power reactors, designs for utilization of the heat with greater thermal efficiency might have received much more research and development support. Similarly, if current controversies over the siting of power plants had been anticipated, concentrated research might have focused on an accelerated development in this country of long-distance transmission technology. High-voltage direct-current lines of 1,000-mile length, or greater, are viewed by many engineers as an eventual solution to siting problems, since they would open up many new alternative possibilities. But the financing necessary to develop this technology has been limited, and such long-distance transmission lines, while technologically feasible, have not been generally accepted by the utilities in the United States as an alternative to extra-high voltage (EHV) and relatively short-haul transmission—which *has* received intensive development in the last decade.[2]

Assessment procedures are likewise needed at the level of technological application. Such procedures could have prevented such commitments as the land acquisition and pre-permit construction investment of the NYSE&G which, as we have seen, may tend to influence the course of events. In assessing technological applications, policy-makers are often faced with making decisions concerning issues which are the subject of public controversy, a situation in which no outcome can

[2] Long-distance underground lines present a more difficult technical problem, but with additional research they could be developed.

be attractive to all concerned. The choice, in this case, is between the conflicting needs for increased power and for environmental protection. There is often only inconclusive scientific information on which to base evaluation of the consequences of each choice. And, in the Bell Station case, we have seen that whatever clarity was provided by scientific attention to the problem tended to be diminished by both company management and its critics in their eagerness to support their own points of view.

We are dealing, then, with political questions. An important factor is the limited constraints on the decision-making power of American industry. Traditionally, in this country, corporations have been able to make major decisions concerning technological application, with little or no restrictions beyond those imposed by market considerations of competition and consumer demand; and market constraints have, to a degree, been manipulable. Even regulated industries, such as utilities, whose rate structure is set outside the industry, have had a great deal of power to control their pattern of growth, and their decisions have contributed to the diminishing capacity of the environment to accommodate the dimensions of economic growth. The NYSE&G made their initial investment with the expectation that there would be little constraint on their independence to determine the design of Bell Station. It is questionable whether this degree of independence is appropriate; for effective monitoring of natural resources requires a distribution of political and decision-making power. The importance of this case, therefore, lies not so much in the effect of one power plant on Cayuga Lake as in the precedents established concerning the power of an industry to lay claim to the use of a scarce resource.

One may conclude that solutions to the problems posed by the Bell Station controversy will require fundamental reconsideration of major institutional patterns in our society. Institutional change is influenced more by political strength than by rational debate, which has demonstrable limits in resolving value conflicts. In this light, an extremely important effect of the controversy was the generation of citizen activity. The agitating by the CSCL and citizens' groups succeeded in jolting what Charles Frankel has called the "public passive voice, . . . created specifically for the conduct of correspondence between a government and its citizens, . . . in which thoughts and emotions float around without belonging to anyone, in which decisions are always in process but are never made, and in which the buck, when it is passed, is passed unerringly into the void." [3]

It is in sharpening awareness of the need for institutional change that the increasing "clout" of technological critics, demonstrated by the influence of the CSCL and its supporting scientists, assumes its importance. In fact, the new alliances and power groups formed around cases such as that of Cayuga Lake, may be their most significant long-range effect.

[3] Charles Frankel, *High on Foggy Bottom* (New York: Harper and Row, 1968), p. 3.

A Note on the Program on Science, Technology, and Society

This case study is the first of a series developed by the Cornell University Program on Science, Technology, and Society, an interdisciplinary program established in the summer of 1969 to stimulate teaching and research on problems relating to the interaction of science and technology with society. The program evolved from a concern with how scientific discovery and technological innovation are changing the functioning of economic and political institutions and the values that influence our social behavior. Its teaching and research activities deal with these concerns in an interdisciplinary framework. The program is funded by the National Science Foundation, the Sloan Foundation, the Henry Luce Foundation, and Cornell University.

The case study series is being developed within the program to fill the need for instructional and public information materials on the social, political, and economic consequences of science and technology and on the ways in which decisions about them are made. Each study will deal with a specific case selected to reveal the complexity of actual situations in which the problems and challenges of technology are an issue. Detailed analysis will be directed to revealing relationships and processes which have implications beyond the individual case.

A number of common themes will be emphasized throughout the series: the use of science and technology to meet public needs, incentives and constraints on the direction of scientific and technological development, and the control of unintended and undesirable consequences of science and technology. We will consider, in relation to each of these themes, the social and political behavior of various groups: scientists and technologists in the political-governmental system acting in situations which carry them beyond their technical expertise; legislators and policy makers, forced to make decisions often on the basis of inconclusive evidence; and the public, concerned with the implications of technology, whose interest and activities are likely to bear increasingly on public policy.

FRANKLIN A. LONG, Director
RAYMOND BOWERS, Deputy Director

Definitions

Epilimnion—the upper layer of a thermally stratified lake.

Eutrophication—the process by which a lake ages with increasing biological activity.

Flushing time—the time required for a drop of water to pass from the source of a lake to its outlet.

Hypolimnion—the bottom and coldest layer of a thermally stratified lake.

Isothermal—of uniform temperature throughout.

Metalimnion—the middle layer of rapid temperature change in a thermally stratified lake.

Plume—the stream of discharge water from a power station.

Thermal pollution—the common term for the disposal of waste heat into cooling water.

Thermocline—a level in a thermally stratified lake at which the maximum rate of temperature change occurs. It serves as a barrier beyond which thermal mixing ceases.

Abbreviations

CAL—Cornell Aeronautical Laboratory
CLBB—Cayuga Lake Basin Regional Water Resources Planning Board
CLPA—Cayuga Lake Preservation Association
Cornell WRC—Cornell Water Resources and Marine Sciences Center
CSCL—Citizens Committee to Save Cayuga Lake
FWPCA—Federal Water Pollution Control Administration
NYSE&G—New York State Electric and Gas Corporation
PSC—Public Service Commission
USAEC *or* AEC—United States Atomic Energy Commission
WRC—State Water Resources Commission

Index

NUCLEAR POWER
AND ITS CRITICS

Designed by R. E. Rosenbaum.
Composed by Vail-Ballou Press, Inc.,
in 11 pt. Linotype Janson 3 points leaded,
with display lines in Monotype Deepdene.
Printed letterpress from type by Vail-Ballou Press
on Warren's No. 66, 60 lb. basis,
with the Cornell University Press watermark.
Bound by Vail-Ballou Press
in Interlaken Pallium bookcloth
and stamped in All Purpose foil.